THE PARK VILLAGE SISTERHOOD

No. 17 Park Village West

The Park Village Sisterhood

THOMAS JAY WILLIAMS
AND
ALLAN WALTER CAMPBELL

LONDON
S·P·C·K
1965

First published in 1965
by S.P.C.K.
Holy Trinity Church
Marylebone Road
London N.W.1

Printed in Great Britain by
Richard Clay (The Chaucer Press), Ltd., Bungay, Suffolk

DEDICATION

TO THE MEMORY OF

SISTER FIDELIA OF
THE DIVINE SILENCE
C. L. J.

OF THE SOCIETY OF THE MOST HOLY TRINITY
WITHOUT WHOSE
ENCOURAGEMENT AND CO-OPERATION
THE HISTORY OF HER SOCIETY
COULD NOT HAVE BEEN WRITTEN

Contents

Illustrations

Preface

The present work is an expansion, in the light of knowledge acquired since 1950, of the chapters of the biography of Priscilla Lydia Sellon, published in that year,[1] in which was related the story, so far as it was then known, of the first Community of the Anglican Revival, the Sisterhood of the Holy Cross. Founded in 1845 at No. 17 Park Village West, Regent's Park, London, this Community was known from its earliest days as "The Park Village Sisterhood". Hence the title of this book.[2]

The sources of information concerning the Park Village Sisterhood available to the author at the time when *Priscilla Lydia Sellon* was being written (1933–47) were for the most part secondary. Foremost among them was H. P. Liddon's *Life of E. B. Pusey*, especially Volume III, and Miss Maria Trench's anonymous *Story of Dr Pusey's Life*. With the exception of quotations from contemporary letters in the pages of these works, the nearest approach to first-hand sources then available was in the autobiographies of an ex-novice of the Park Village Community, Margaret Anna Cusack. The first of these, entitled *Five Years in a Protestant Sisterhood and Ten Years in a Catholic Convent*, was published anonymously in 1869, when the author's fervour as a convert to the Roman Catholic Church was at its highest. In the second, entitled *The Nun of Kenmare*, published in 1888 under her name in Religion, Sister Mary Frances Clare (although she had left the Roman Catholic Church and abandoned the Religious Life), she displays less bitterness towards her two

---

[1] *Priscilla Lydia Sellon: The Restorer after Three Hundred Years of the Religious Life in the English Church.* By Thomas Jay Williams (S.P.C.K. 1950, revised edition in preparation).

[2] This precedent of designating a Religious Community by the name of its location has been followed in the case of almost all the older Communities of both men and women in the English Church: "Wantage", for the Community of St Mary the Virgin whose mother-house is in that town; "Devonport" or "Ascot", for the Society of the Most Holy Trinity; "Clewer", for the Community of St John Baptist; "East Grinstead", for the Society of St Margaret; "Cowley", for the Society of St John the Evangelist; "Mirfield", for the Community of the Resurrection; "Kelham", for the Society of the Sacred Mission; "Nashdom", for the Anglican Order of St Benedict.

former allegiances (Anglican and Roman Catholic) than is manifest
in her "swan-song" of hatred towards them both, *The Story of my
Life*, published in 1899, the year of her death.[1] There is mention of
the Park Village Sisterhood of the Holy Cross and of some of the
Sisters in Miss Margaret Goodman's *Sisterhoods in the Church of
England*; also casual references in Miss E. J. Whately's *Maude* (1878,
reissued in 1895 under its original sub-title, *The Anglican Sister of
Mercy*) and in the attacks on Mother Lydia and the Devonport
Society by the Rev. Messrs. Colles and Cookesley, in their respective
pamphlets, *Sisters of Mercy, Sisters of Misery*, and *An Open Letter
to His Grace the Archbishop of Dublin*. There are references also in
the columns of the Church press in 1850 and 1851, in letters of Mr
Dodsworth and Bishop Blomfield, and in Dr Pusey's rejoinders,
especially in his *Renewed Explanation in Consequence of Mr Dodsworth's Letter to the Bishop of London*. There is a brief but important
reference to one of the first Sisters in a letter of Dr Pusey quoted in
Canon Perry's *George Hay Forbes: A Romance in Scholarship* (page
27).

A letter received from Mr Allan W. Campbell a few weeks after
the appearance of *Priscilla Lydia Sellon*, confirming the tentative
identification of Miss Colt, the lady referred to in the aforementioned
letter, marked the beginning of a correspondence between the author
and Mr Campbell which soon developed into a partnership in research, yielding a rich harvest of knowledge of the history, personnel,
and habitats of the Park Village Sisterhood. Census returns, death
certificates, wills, thanks to Mr Campbell, his sister-in-law, Mrs Stella
Campbell, and Miss Mavis Mackinnon have supplied many important,
interesting, and sometimes surprising details. The discovery by Mr

---

[1] Copies of *The Nun of Kenmare* and *The Story of my Life* can still be found on the
shelves of second-hand bookshops or in the catalogues of public libraries. *Five Years*
is harder to come by. There is a copy in the Library of the British Museum, and there
are at least two copies in the United States: in the Boston Public Library and the New
York Society Library. The book is not only anonymous as to authorship, but pseudo-
nyms and initials are used throughout to designate the "leading characters" and the
places mentioned. Mother Lydia (Miss Sellon) appears as "Miss Jones", Dr Pusey as
"Dr Smithson", London is "Helston", Park Village West and Osnaburgh Street share
the name "Helston Street", Plymouth is "Westernmere". The Sisters are designated
by the initials of their family or Christian names: Miss Ellacombe is "Miss E."; Sister
Anne Terrot is usually "A." or "Sister A.", once, "Miss T."; Child Clara (Miss Powell)
is "Child C.", Miss Ogilvie (Sister Katherine) is "Miss O.", Mother Emma Langston
is thinly disguised as "Miss Langton".

Campbell of the collections of letters to and from Dr Pusey relating to the early days of the Sisterhood, copied for the use of Dr Liddon in the preparation of his monumental *Life* of Dr Pusey and stored on the shelves of the library of Pusey House, Oxford, opened up new and valuable sources of contemporary information. Thanks to the labours of one of the members of the Society of St Francis, the pamphlets, tracts, and like printed matter have since been catalogued and made more intelligently accessible for research. The painstaking work of Mr Campbell, the Reverend Father Pulley, s.s.j.e., and Mr Robert Cover, made available enough fresh information to justify the writing of a separate monograph on the Park Village Sisterhood. Further researches at both Pusey House and Ascot Priory by the author in the summers of 1960, 1961, 1962, 1963, 1964, brought to light even more information, long forgotten, which, added to the material made available by the aforesaid collaborators, has made possible the approximately complete story of the Park Village Sisterhood recorded in the body of this work.

The researches at Pusey House and at Ascot Priory would not have been possible had it not been for the co-operation of the Principal and Custodian of the one, and the generous trust of the Warden and Reverend Mother Superior of the other, in giving the author every facility for the study of the materials in their respective custody.

Another source of information to which I wish to express my grateful indebtedness is a reference in the notes on the revival of conventual life in the Anglican Communion appended to the privately printed memoir of the late Mother Annie Louisa of the Community of St Mary the Virgin, Wantage. This reference provided a definite clue to the hitherto baffling identification of the Sister of the Park Village Sisterhood, referred to by Miss Cusack as "Miss O.", who was anointed in her last illness by a "very High Church bishop", as Katherine Ogilvie. The identification of the said bishop as Alexander Penrose Forbes, Bishop of the Scottish Episcopalian See of Brechin, had already been established beyond reasonable doubt. To the evidence for the identification of "Miss O." with the anointing bishop's kinswoman, Katherine Ogilvie, presented in an article in *Holy Cross Magazine* (West Park, New York) of April 1956, entitled *A Lost Treasure Retrieved*, there has since been added a contemporary statement in the diary of Mother Marian Hughes that Bishop Forbes was in Oxford, visiting Dr Pusey, in June 1850, the month and year of Sister Katherine's death. The hour of Sister Katherine's death is recorded in Sister Margaret Esther's notes on Park Village made accessible to one of the authors by the Reverend Mother Superior of the Community of St John Baptist, Clewer. To Mother Emma Langston's nephew, Mr C. Langston of Chilgrove, Ashtead, the authors are indebted for information about her family. This information, with further data gathered from the letters of Mr Dodsworth to Dr Pusey, and the letter of the Reverend James Isaacson, introducing Miss Langston to Dr Pusey and from Miss Langston herself to Dr. Pusey before her coming to London with mention of the place, but not the date, of her death in the records at Ascot Priory, have been incorporated into the text of this history.

Much valuable information about the formative period in the institution of conventual life in the English Church was made available by the painstaking work of Sister Catherine, s.h.u.t., in deciphering and copying page after page of Dr Pusey's letters to Miss (later Mother) Marian Hughes and copying from Mother Marian's diaries and the annals of her Society an account of Miss Hughes' share in the inauguration of the Sisterhood which she was herself not able to join at the time of its foundation.

To the Reverend Edward Rochie Hardy, ph.d., d.d., th.d., Professor of Ecclesiastical History in Berkeley Divinity School, New Haven, Connecticut, U.S.A., I am indebted not only for the Introduction which he has provided for the present work but also for many suggestions and criticisms which have made the book less unworthy of his commendation.

I also wish to express my gratitude to the Editorial Staff of the Society for Promoting Christian Knowledge, the publishers of this work, for the patience, courtesy, and personal kindness which have marked their association with the authors.

Most of all I am indebted to my collaborator, Mr Campbell, whose name I am honoured to have inscribed along with my own as co-author of this history of *The Park Village Sisterhood*, and to the late Sister Fidelia, c.l.j., to whose memory this work is dedicated.

Retreat House of the Redeemer,   THOMAS JAY WILLIAMS
New York.
Epiphany 1965.

Introduction

Two periods in the reign of Queen Victoria are marked by significant propaganda for radical social changes, followed some years later by the achievement of concrete reforms. Parallel with the Chartist agitation of the 1840s and the activities of the Fabian Society in the 1890s there was in each case within the Church of England a new appreciation of its corporate nature and its social mission. In the former case this is connected with the Christian Socialism of Frederick Denison Maurice, in the latter with the rising influence of Charles Gore. Not unconnected with these more conspicuous movements was in each of these periods a new departure in the revival of monastic institutions in Anglicanism. Mirfield, Kelham, and the Society of the Divine Compassion began in the 1890s, and in the 1840s the early Sisterhoods, the story of the first of which is told in this volume. The three Brotherhoods mentioned, of which two still flourish while the other has served God in its generation and passed away, were all in the minds of their early members definitely related to the changing needs created by the changing social patterns of the day. Gore is related to all three phenomena, as Christian socialist (or at least social Christian), theologian, and monastic founder. One cannot find so close a connection in the earlier period. Maurice had only an external interest in Sisterhoods[1]—although the saying ascribed to him that those who believe in the Holy Communion ought to be Holy Communists should have attracted his attention to these intense expressions of the common life in Christ. Pusey seems at first sight more disposed to defy than to consecrate the trends of the times. Still less were the unpretentious Sisters of Park Village West aware of any more sophisticated vocation than the worship of God and the service of his poor. But there are interconnections nevertheless. Pusey's ministry was the most "socially conscious" of the Tractarian group, as strikingly connected with meeting the needs of sufferers from cholera epidemics

---

[1] Cf. his rather abstract opinion quoted in A. M. Allchin, *The Silent Rebellion*, 1958, p. 125.

as with expounding the faith in University Sermons. The imperial-istic schemes of Priscilla Lydia Sellon certainly express a desire to relate the Church to the world as well as a call to leave the world for the cloister. And on the list of sponsors of the original Park Village enterprise, which contemporaries were doubtless reassured to see headed by the name of a duke's son and several peers, we are probably more interested to notice the name of the rising young Tory politi-cian, as he then was, William Ewart Gladstone. Indeed Gladstone is for this period the parallel to Gore, since the range of his interests did extend over theology (with a special interest in the relations of Church and State), politics, and monastic institutions, as Gore's did fifty years later.

Some of these ramifications of the Anglican monastic revival have been explored in Fr Williams' previous work on the life of Mother Lydia[1], and in A. M. Allchin's interpretative study of *The Silent Rebellion*. There is always an element of divine paradox in the life of the cloister. It is brought into contact with the world by the very fact of withdrawal into the intimacy of the love of God—there is, I imagine, a certain smiling resignation in St Benedict's observation that guests are never lacking in a monastery.[2] The Sisters of the Holy Cross were part of a larger picture than any of them were probably aware of, except perhaps during the dramatic episode of the nursing mission to the Crimean War which was both the greatest hour of their little community and also the immediate cause of its dissolution. It is, however, primarily the intimate rather than the outreaching aspect of their story which is here presented with loving care. Fr Williams has unearthed a surprising amount of detailed information about the various members of the Park Village Sisterhood; we are probably justified in saying that he has here recorded as much about them as is ever likely to be known on earth. This was after all the first Anglican religious community to come into indubitable existence as such, after the series of *monai*, from Little Gidding to Littlemore, which had approached the principle without quite reaching it. Angli-can *pietas* is enough to justify making while it is still possible to do so the fullest record of its life from beginning to end. The result, moreover, is a very human story, which like all good stories has a beginning, a middle, and an end, and like many of them has a prologue

---

[1] *Priscilla Lydia Sellon* (S.P.C.K. 1950).
[2] *Regula Sancti Benedicti*, chapter 53.

and an epilogue. There is the preparation for the idea, its realization in Park Village West, its expansion in Osnaburgh Street, its explosion to the Crimea, and then the end of the Park Village community as a separate entity. The epilogue is death, but since this is a Christian story death is followed by resurrection. What happened in 1856 was formally an absorption of the Sisterhood of the Holy Cross into the Devonport Society of Sisters of Mercy, the Society of the Most Holy Trinity thus being formed. But Ascot Priory to-day continues both traditions, and indeed its life of contemplation overflowing into unpretentious service is perhaps closer to the spirit of the early Park Village community than to the life of activity supported by prayer which was the quality of the early years at Devonport. The latter is carried on more by some of the more active communities than by the direct spiritual descendants of the early "Sellonites".[1]

In contrast with the broader scope of the life of Mother Lydia, the detailed story of the first Sisterhood which is here told moves with an almost Aristotelian unity—it is the story of a few people serving God for a few years in a few streets in the district of St Pancras, interrupted by a message from the distant Scythian Chersonese. This was the day of little things; Mother Lydia was speaking in terms of the scale of early foundations when she referred to the seven ladies then at Osnaburgh Street as "a large Sisterhood in London".[1] But this is a story of small-scale exemplifications of large issues. From these early experiences Anglican monastic founders learned lessons which had to be learned, some of them the hard way even though they were already written in the book of monastic history. One, as Dr Pusey himself later observed, was that a community could not be solidly established without an adequate head; poor Mother Emma showed well enough that she did not have the gifts of a Mother Superior, let alone those of a Foundress. Another was the ancient principle that even ascetic enthusiasm must be informed by the saving grace of discretion. Sister Katherine Ogilvie's fatal Lenten fast on a dish of coarse oatmeal taken after Compline was a tragic effort to renew the rigours of the Thebaid in Victorian London. But most important of all was the gradual discovery that, when the Anglican world was barely prepared to welcome and support "Sisters of Mercy", God was calling some of his children in *Ecclesia Anglicana* to the harder and

[1] See p. 89 below.

lonelier way of contemplation as well. Mr Dodsworth's remark that "nothing has ever been *simply restored*", and that we would not again have nuns, though we might have something like them,[1] was both true and false. We do have nuns, and in fact they came very soon in Mother Lydia's "Second Order", in which one sees the primary continuation of the Park Village foundation. In recent years Communities even more strictly contemplative have developed. But on the other hand no absolute restoration of a past age was either possible or desirable in the monastic revival any more than in the Catholic movement generally, or for that matter in the architectural revivals of the period. Even when old principles come to life in a new age they are necessarily expressed somewhat differently. The vitality of the monastic calling, like that of other Christian vocations, is shown by the very fact that its expressions are not static and its solutions are not permanent. Various problems are still being worked out which are not destined to receive a final and unchanging solution. One is the relation of action and contemplation in the mixed life—in which it must be remembered, and not by those technically "religious" alone, that, as St Thomas Aquinas so well put it, action should be something added to contemplation and not something taken away from it.[2] Another is the practical problem what active works are best carried on by religious communities, and in what areas it may be better for Sisterhoods or Brotherhoods to pioneer and leave others to carry on as a vocation of its own in the life of society what they have begun, as has happened conspicuously with nursing. These are only examples; in the words of the Psalmist, "I see that all things come to an end; but thy commandment is exceeding broad" (Psalm 119. 96).

So there are many ways in which the intimate story of the Sisterhood of the Holy Cross could be fitted into larger contexts. It is part of the renewed vitality of Anglicanism at large. It is, though less conspicuously than the life of some other Sisterhoods, part of the expansion of women's activities beyond the family into the public sphere. But above all, this early community was a religious house, and it is as such that it should be remembered. Its true success, if the term may be used, is known to God alone. But I find the external sign of it in the quiet lives of the Sisters "of the old foundation" who

---

[1] (Maria Trench), *The Story of Dr Pusey's Life*, p. 274; see p. 32 below.
[2] *Summa Theologica* II, II, 182, 1 *ad tert.*

found a life-long vocation in holy religion for almost two generations of the life of the world, until the last survivor of Park Village died at Ascot Priory in the present century. One may certainly apply to the Sisters of the Holy Cross what the modern historian of the English Benedictines has written with reference to his own confreres:

> The true monk, in whatever century he is found, looks not to the changing ways around him or to his own mean condition, but to the unchanging everlasting God, and his trust is in the everlasting arms that hold him. Christ's words are true: He who doth not renounce all that he possesseth cannot be my disciple. His promise also is true: He that followeth me walketh not in darkness, but shall have the light of life.[1]

Berkeley Divinity School.   EDWARD ROCHIE HARDY
Feast of the Holy Name, 1961.

---

[1] David Knowles, *The Religious Orders in England*, Vol. III, 1959, p. 468.

B

I

The Background and Beginning of the First Sisterhood
1844—1845

The Church of England as one knows it to-day represents the medieval Church as affected by four influences: the Reformation of the sixteenth century, the Laudian Revival of the seventeenth, the Evangelical Movement of the eighteenth, and the Oxford Movement of the nineteenth. This book is concerned with an enterprise which owes something to all four of these movements, but was primarily a product of the last. The medieval Religious Communities disappeared in the reign of Henry VIII as a result of the Act of 1536, dissolving the communities and supressing the monastic life of both men and women. There were a few revived foundations under Mary I, but these ended with her reign. For nearly three centuries thereafter the Religious Life was the subject of occasional theoretical, and fewer still sporadic practical, essays at revival. These discussions and abortive practical efforts have been summarized by the Reverend Edmund E. Seyzinger, c.r., in his preface to the first edition of *Priscilla Lydia Sellon.*

The impulse which led to the establishment of Religious Communities as a recognized feature of Anglicanism came ultimately from Keble's Assize Sermon of 1833, although the poet Robert Southey, in 1829, had advocated the revival of "Sisters of Charity" as social workers among the poor. The life of Religion in the technical sense was thought of as something exclusively Roman Catholic. Precedents of a sort might have been found among some of the Lutheran Churches of Germany, where a few Sisterhoods had survived the Reformation in altered forms, and even in Lutheran Denmark, where houses for unmarried ladies of good family existed, as they still exist,

1

under the name of "cloister" and under the rule of a "Prioress". There is no evidence that the Tractarian leaders were aware of these facts. They would in any case have been averse to the following of Protestant models. The Religious Life was revived in the Church of England as a part of a campaign for asserting the full Catholic character of that Church. At that time, and for long after, foreign Protestant Communities were viewed with indifference, if not hostility, by orthodox Churchmen. It is only in the present day that some balanced appreciation has been possible of the *vestigia ecclesiae* which have survived the most discouraging circumstances.

A more relevant survival, but one which seems to have been equally unknown to the promoters of the conventual revival in the English Church, was the Royal Hospital of St Katherine, which had stood in Regent's Park since 1826. This was founded, probably in 1147, by Matilda, the Queen of King Stephen, for the maintenance of thirteen poor persons, and for the benefit of her own soul and the souls of her husband and children. As reported to the Charity Commission in 1837 the establishment consisted then, as provided by the Statutes, of the Master (a retired General who had been private secretary to King George III and Queen Charlotte), three Brothers, one of whom was in Holy Orders, and three Sisters. The Master's stipend was £1,200 per Year, the Brothers received £300 each, the Sisters £200 each. The Royal Foundation of St Katherine's Hospital is of no more than antiquarian interest to-day to those concerned with the history of the revival of the Religious Life in the English Church. But it might easily have been restored as a genuine Religious Community, and so have been the nucleus of an official, rather than a private, enterprise, as was the actual case with the conventual revival of the nineteenth century.[1]

The first Anglican Religious professed under a vow of Religion was Miss Marian Rebecca Hughes, who took a vow of celibacy at Oxford on Trinity Sunday, 6 June 1841, four years before the foun-

---

[1] It may be doubted, however, if such official revival would have taken the distinctly monastic form which marked it from the beginning in Park Village West and has continued so to distinguish its development. The actual development of the Royal Foundation of St Katherine's Hospital has, in recent years, been along sound Catholic sociological lines, nearer the site of the original foundation, in what is now East London, than the aristocratic atmosphere of the Regent's Park of the early eighteen hundreds. (See note quoting Mr Peter F. Anson on page 20 below.)

dation of the Park Village Sisterhood in 1845, and eight years before the initiation in 1849 of her own Community, the Society of the Holy and Undivided Trinity. On 19 April 1842 John Henry Newman founded at Littlemore, a suburb of Oxford, an "embryo-monastery", where he and some of his friends and disciples lived in community. This establishment came to an end and in 1845, the year of the founding of the first Sisterhood, Mr Newman and many of its members were received into the Roman Catholic Church. On 24 August 1842, four months after community life began at Littlemore, the American Episcopal Church produced rather prematurely a male community at Nashotah in what at that time was part of the Western Territory, which was not admitted as a State of the Union until 1848. The Nashotah Community consisted partly of clergy and partly of students. Its aim was to evangelize the Middle West and to train priests for frontier work. By 1850 Nashotah House had lost its monastic character. It has survived various vicissitudes to become one of the smaller leading theological seminaries of the American Episcopal Church of to-day. These two communities—Littlemore and the Nashotah Mission—proved to be as transitory as the pre-Tractarian attempts at the revival of monastic life. It was left to the "devout female sex" to establish the first Religious Community which really struck root in Anglican soil.

The idea of establishing Religious Communities in the Church of England seems to have been first raised in practical terms in a letter from Dr Pusey to the Reverend William Farquhar Hook, D.D., Vicar of Leeds, dated December 1839.

> I want very much to have one or more societies of *Sœurs de la Charité* formed: I think them desirable: (1) in themselves as belonging to and fostering a high tone in the Church; (2) as giving a holy employment to many who yearn for something; (3) as directing zeal, which will otherwise go off in some irregular way, or go over to Rome. . . . It seems best that at first they should not be discursive, as those of the Romish Church in Ireland, but be employed in hospitals, lunatic asylums, prisons, among the females. Do you know any who would engage in it on a small scale, quietly, or one who would be a Mother Superior, i.e., one fitted to guide it?

In the same month in which he had written to Dr Hook, Dr Pusey wrote to Mr Keble to the same effect as to Dr Hook, saying that Newman and he had arrived at the idea simultaneously. He had named it, he told Mr Keble, to very different sorts of persons. All were taken with it exceedingly, except the chaplain to the Archbishop of Canterbury, who was "half afraid of it". Newman himself wrote on 21 February 1840:

> Pusey is at present very eager about setting up Sisters of Mercy.... I despair of such societies being *made* externally. They must be the expression of an inward principle. All one can do is to offer the opportunity. I am sceptical, too, whether they can be set up without a quasi-vow.

This was fair comment. But even Newman does not seem to have appreciated the difficulty of starting at the beginning with a Superior who had not herself made a novitiate under expert guidance. Ultimately, on 9 June 1840, Dr Hook wrote to Dr Pusey endorsing the proposal to establish Sisters of Charity, but pointing out the risk of opposition from managing "Evangelical" ladies, and advising discretion:

> What I should like to have done is this: for you to train an elderly matron, full of zeal, and thoroughly imbued with right principles, and for her to come [to Leeds] and take lodgings with two or three other females. Let their object be known to none but myself.... We should attend to their *principles*, but draw up no rules, except such as might be absolutely necessary for the guidance of the household, and there should be no distinction of dress....

The Sisters would work on an experimental basis for twelve months, and then rules would be drawn up and an unobtrusive form of distinguishing dress decided upon.

Much of this advice was sound, but the situation was developing too quickly. Newman in his series of essays published in the same year, *The Church of the Fathers*, suggested publicly that "there was no reason why the Church of England should not, from among its members, supply those requisites" which were necessary for "the life and character of a Sister of Mercy". This book was read by at least two young women (both in Gloucestershire) in whom it awakened a desire to dedicate themselves to God in the virgin state. One of these was Miss Marian Rebecca Hughes, the daughter of a Gloucestershire priest. The other was Miss Jane Isabella Ellacombe, a daughter of the one-time noted campanologist, Henry Thomas Ellacombe, Vicar of Bitton, a life-long friend of both Newman and Pusey. Miss Hughes recorded in her diary that as a consequence of reading the passage from *The Church of the Fathers* cited above: "I resolved to dedicate my life, by God's grace, and thus to prepare for the Day of Judgment." She gave up wearing jewellery, sold her jewels, and wrote anonymously to Mr Newman, sending the money realized from the sale and telling him of her desire to dedicate her life, and asking his prayers.

In 1841 Miss Hughes spoke of her desire to be a Sister of Mercy to an Oxford priest, the Reverend Charles Seager, with whom she was acquainted through her cousin, the Reverend Thomas Chamberlain, Vicar of the Church of St Thomas the Martyr, Oxford. From him she learned that no steps had as yet been taken to establish a Sisterhood, although there was a strong desire for it in the minds of the writers of the *Tracts for the Times*. Mr Seager, who taught elementary Hebrew, was in consequence acquainted with the Professor of Hebrew, who was Dr Pusey himself. He told Dr Pusey of Miss Hughes' aspiration. Dr Pusey welcomed this approach. His own daughter, Lucy, hoped to be a Religious and, although in her early 'teens, had already inspired several young women of her acquaintance, some older than herself, and others her own schoolmates, with a like desire.

Dr Pusey arranged for Miss Hughes to make her Profession on the day when Lucy was to make her First Communion, in the University Church of St Mary the Virgin, of which Newman was vicar. Early in the morning of Trinity Sunday, 6 June 1841, Dr Pusey sent the following letter to Mr Newman:

Christ Church, Trinity Sunday, 1841

My dear Friend,
A young lady who is very grateful for your teaching is purposing to-day to take a vow of holy celibacy. She has difficulties and anxieties in her position. She has attended St Mary's since she has been in Oxford, and hopes to receive the Holy Communion there to-day as part of her self-devotion. It was wished that you should know it and remember her. You will know her by her being dressed in white with an ivory cross. . . .
Yours very gratefully and affectionately,
E. B. PUSEY

The service for the Consecration of a Virgin in the Roman Pontifical was celebrated in Mr Seager's house and it may be presumed that Pusey was the officiant. At the point in the service where Mass is celebrated and the newly Professed makes her Communion, there was an adjournment to St Mary's Church. Newman there celebrated the Holy Communion for the general congregation. Many years afterwards Miss Hughes herself described the scene in a letter to Dr Pusey's youngest daughter, Mrs Brine:

> I made my Communion by the side of your sister Lucy . . . and of Lady Lucy [Dr Pusey's mother] and Dr Pusey. In those days all remained in their seats around the chancel, and Dr Newman brought to each the Blessed Sacrament.

There was still no immediate prospect of founding a Religious Community, although the Church of England now had its first Professed Religious, since she was kept at home to look after her parents. In September 1841 she went to Normandy with Mr Seager and his wife to collect information about the Religious Life. She visited an Ursuline Convent in Bayeux and the Convent of the Visitation at Caen and studied their Rules. "Pusey was much interested in these details and in such information as Mr Seager could collect about the conditions under which temporary vows were allowed in the French Church."

In the same year Dr Pusey visited Ireland, accompanied by his children. He took Lucy to visit several convents. He "expressed the wish to witness the ceremony of a Religious Profession", and made contact with the Superior of the Irish Sisters of Charity, whose Community had been founded in 1815 for the relief and visitation of the sick poor. The Superior invited Dr Pusey to a Profession in the Mother House in Stanhope Street, Dublin, "on which occasion his respectful demeanour and recollected manner much struck those who observed him".

The immediate impulse which finally led to the foundation of the first Sisterhood came with Southey's death on 21 March 1843. On 17 November Lord John Manners, afterwards Duke of Rutland, wrote a letter which was published in *The English Churchman*, at that time a Tractarian journal, of 23 November, and it was reprinted in *The Morning Post* of 25 November. This letter took up the matter of erecting a monument to Southey's memory and expressed the hope that "national gratitude would decree to Southey a commemoration more in accordance with his own Christian feelings". He pointed out that Southey's principal object was "restoring to the Church of England the power of watching over and caring for the desolate and needy, which the accidents of the Reformation, in some measure, at least, deprived her of". The destitution of London itself was "clinging in its painful rankness, as it were, to the very walls of our Mother Church, and shaming the magnificence of the rising palace of Westminster". Southey's best monument, to "commemorate the dead, and benefit the living, . . would be a house of Sisters of Mercy. Of course, not without the direct sanction of the Bishop of the diocese and the Metropolitan". Lord John concluded by asking the editors to receive the names of those willing to subscribe to the erection of such a monument to Southey's memory. In an editorial note *The Morning Post* agreed to this.

Lucy Pusey died of tuberculosis on 22 April 1844, having been charged by her father on her death-bed "to pray in the presence of her Redeemer for the institutions 'to which she had hoped to belong' ". On the day of her funeral two letters were written to Dr Pusey reporting on two meetings which had been held in London to discuss the establishment of a Sisterhood, as the result of Lord John's public appeal for a Southey memorial house. In later years Lord John described the first meeting as follows:

> The origin of the first Sisterhood of Mercy in the Church of England was as follows: Southey had forcibly and persistently advocated the establishment in England of institutions resembling the Beguinages of the Low Countries. When he died, there was much discussion in the papers as to the form his memorial should take. I suggested in a letter to *The Morning Post*, the chief Church paper of that day, a Sisterhood of Mercy; the suggestion was favourably received. A few people met in my rooms in The Albany, and it was determined to start the enterprise, subject to two conditions—First, that it should be located in a parish whose incumbent would welcome it and become its spiritual head; and, second, that it should receive the sanction of the Bishop of the diocese. The first was fulfilled by Mr Dodsworth, Vicar of Christ Church, St Pancras, accepting the post, and the second in the way described in a note taken at the time: "Had an interview with the Bishop of London [Blomfield] about the Sisters of Mercy, at which he said it was dangerous at such times as ours to propose such a scheme. . . . But after discussing the chief points and agreeing on most of them, he said he would consult the Archbishop, and so the matter rested for a couple of months, and he has now written me a letter which I think will authorize us to proceed."

The second meeting (held on the day of Lucy Pusey's funeral) was attended by Lord John Manners and other prominent laymen and also by Dr Hook, whose sister at this time aspired to the Religious Life, and the Reverend William Dodsworth, vicar of Christ Church, Albany Street. Mr Gladstone, then President of the Board of Trade and a member of the Cabinet, was unable to attend but "wrote in warm sympathy with the object of the meeting". He made himself responsible for the greater part of the financial support of the undertaking, and when a "confidential" circular was issued, notifying interested persons of the proposed venture, "the document was drafted by Mr Gladstone and set down in his own handwriting".

"One of the two letters to Dr Pusey was from Lord John Manners, officially communicating the result of the deliberations of (the second) meeting. Dr Hook had urged that a Lady Superior must first of all be found, since the initiative and plan of procedure must first come from her who was to work it; and Lord John Manners had been instructed by the meeting to ask Pusey whether he knew of any person who was qualified for such a post. . . . the meeting 'had resolved to take preliminary steps for the establishment and permanent maintenance of a Sisterhood living under a religious Rule and engaged in some work of mercy such as

1. Visiting the poor or the sick in their own homes.
2. Visiting hospitals, workhouses, or prisons.
3. Feeding, clothing, and instructing destitute children.
4. Assisting in burying the dead.' "

Welcome as this approach must have been to Dr Pusey, he was unable to suggest a suitable Superior at the moment.

Several young women known to Dr Pusey were looking forward to the establishment of the Sisterhood. The gradual evolution of the plans for it may be traced in letters from Dodsworth to Dr Pusey, now at Pusey House. On Whitsun Eve (25 May 1844) Dodsworth wrote:

It seems to me that whether we begin with two or three or more, we must have a head; otherwise we shall be exposing the Institution to a severer test than is needful. I suppose also that Lord John Manners and others who will exert themselves to provide the means will look for some elements of *permanency* in it. The more simple and unobtrusive it can be made the better. I am inclined to think that there would be *many* applicants which makes it more needful that we should have a competent head. I wish you would undertake to be their spiritual adviser and, so far as may be, confessor. I would thankfully act under your directions, so far as I could properly assist, and the readiness of communication now would make your occasional visits comparatively easy.

Among the aspirants was Miss Jane Ellacombe, of whom mention has already been made. Mr Ellacombe wrote to Dr Pusey in the early summer of 1844 to ask "whether he could not find for his daughter some situation as governess where she would enjoy religious advantages and have full occupation". Two letters in reply to Mr Ellacombe about his daughter's vocation are reproduced in part of Canon Liddon's *Life of E. B. Pusey.*

June 9, 1844.

If as a father, I may write to a father, I would venture to suggest what I should do myself were Jane my child. I cannot doubt that this drawing of people's minds toward a more devoted life, giving themselves to His service, and the ministering to His poor, is ... of God. It has been growing wonderfully during the last years. . . . Some of those who have been led that way (whom I myself know) have been brought to it remarkably. There has, too, been for some years, prayer that God would give us these institutions. . . .

Were I her father, I should certainly not ... abruptly check the feeling which she has so strongly, nor even attempt to divert it, but only try its steadfastness. It seems to me to want guidance and discipline, and this she herself wishes for. A time of probation might be imposed during which she might be living, in your house, and among your poor, something of the sort of life she wishes for hereafter. But I cannot help feeling that a mind so energetic, and so strongly penetrated with this longing might become something which might give you deep pleasure, and be a source of blessing to others. I have myself seen something of this sort among ourselves. Such an institution is actually contemplated in London ... which Lord J. Manners has set on foot: he has conditional approbation of the Bishop . . . . This gives some sort of substance to it. Our authorities permit that the trial should be made. . . .

The subject has been very near to my heart for some years: the daughter, whom it pleased God lately to take to Himself, had chosen that life, and was preparing for it: and I saw in her the healthful influence of looking forward to it. To our Church I am sure it would be a blessing. We have deep needs which Sisters of Charity alone can meet, and which as far as they are met now, being relieved by Roman Catholic institutions, result in withdrawing our poor from us.

> To many ardent minds, like your daughter's, the establishment of Sisterhoods will remove many sore temptations away from our Church and develop higher energies.

The background of Miss Ellacombe's vocation can be traced in correspondence which has survived at Pusey House. On 20 August 1843, she wrote to her father explaining why she had broken off her engagement of marriage:

> I had I believe a sort of abstract admiration of celibacy some time before I was engaged and before it affected me personally, and I used to think a good deal about Sisters of Charity and made rather a rash promise one day when we had been talking about convents with Mr Pearsall and Lucy Ellacombe, in case I ever had a fortune left me, to found one if it should be then thought possible. But this was perhaps more romancing than anything else. . . . Of course without my saying so, you will impute a great deal of all this to the Oxford writings and lay the blame on them and particularly on Mr Newman. . . . You will perhaps blame yourself for not forbidding my reading anything of Newman's, but if you only knew, my dear Papa, all the good his writings have done me, you would encourage me in reading them, rather than the contrary. . . . I should have been much worse than I am now but for his writings under God. Our minds you know are all so different that one person cannot tell what suits another, and there are to me no writings so searching and humbling as his. . . . You asked me whether I wished to go into a Nunnery. I certainly have no such wish at present, nor do I expect ever to wish for an inactive life. Were there such an Institution in our own Church, and were there no stronger claims at home, I might wish to be a Sister of Charity, and this I may as well say at once, now I have said so much, though I have no settled ideas on the subject, nor is there need at present to think about it . . . perhaps you wished to have my reasons for preferring a single life, and not only those which led me to enter upon one. . . . First then, I believe, I have preferred it as being, when religiously undertaken, a higher and holier state in itself—and again one in which one can devote oneself more entirely to Christ's service. . . .

Mr Ellacombe then wrote to Newman, who replied :

> *Littlemore.*
> *August 28, 1843*

My dear Ellacombe,
    Your letter is on the subject of one of the most painful trials which can come upon a father: and though of course I am quite unable and un-

worthy to sympathise with you duly, yet pray let me offer you at least my sincere sorrow such as it is, and my earnest wishes that this unexpected event may end more happily than it has commenced.

I hope it is unnecessary for me to state my conviction that nothing I have written can be adduced in behalf of the breach of a positive engagement.

And it is plain too, that, in the instance of such very solemn feelings as are actuating your daughter, she should be very jealous of herself, lest she is acting under impulse, or in a transitory and accidental frame of mind, which may be no part of herself, and may wear away as she gets older.

On the other hand, I cannot think it would be well for her to fulfil her engagement with such feelings on her mind, which it might make her very miserable afterwards to have neglected. A delay would shew what came of them.

Nor should I be honest, did I not add that, unless a promise had been given to one who has not released her from it, I could not be sorry to know that a young person had given herself to a single life—and I am certain that God would bless her in any humble and cautious resolution to that effect. And I suppose engagements are often dissolved by consent of all parties on reasons short of those of a sacred character.

Surely we cannot be better than in Almighty hands. Our own best devised plans continually fail. We get harm where we expected good. The future is utterly hidden from us. How many sufferings and troubles are there in life reserved for those we love! and who would take into his own hands the destiny of those dearest to him without a call of duty? You indeed are influenced by the most affectionate and fatherly feelings: but bear with me when I say, let God work if it be His will to work— and let us act only when He does not.

Believe me, my dear Ellacombe,

Very truly yours,

JOHN H. NEWMAN

P.S. I will have the passage in my sermon copied out and sent to you.

On 3 September 1843 Miss Ellacombe wrote again to her father at some length:

I am very sorry you should all have had such trouble about the sermon, and that Mr Newman should have been troubled about it too. It is quite a mistake to suppose I attributed breaking off my engagement to it. . . . I believe I considered Mr Newman's story of Demetrias which you now have, as a precedent, though it was not that which first turned me, but texts of scripture. . . .

Dr Pusey's letter of 9 June 1844 seems to have reconciled her father at last to the idea that she might become a Sister. On 14 June Dr Pusey wrote suggesting that she should be prepared by working in her father's parish "upon a plan involving Daily Services". Finally, on 25 July he wrote:

> I have just heard that it is arranged that a house should be taken for Sisters in London, whenever God should make it clear that any are called to it. But at present there is only one ready, and I think that the intervening time will be really a gain in that the individuals will be preparing themselves and understand better how great a preparation of heart is necessary. . . . Should you think hereafter of your daughter joining such an Institution, the individuals who are likely to engage in it at first would be older than herself and of good judgment: the one who is free for it is thirty.

The one who was free was Miss Mary Bruce, who was born in 1814.

In the meantime Dr Pusey was corresponding with Miss Marian Hughes about practical details. Soon after Lucy's death, he wrote to Miss Hughes:

> I write now, immediately, to ask you for any information you can give me in consequence of your residence in Convents. It seems as if we were now to attain one, so mercifully does God give us what we long for in one way, while for our unworthiness He takes it away in ours. I am employed in helping in drawing up some rules and I should be glad to know any results of what you learnt. I think I understand that you wrote something down at the time. . . .

In an undated letter, written probably on 17 August 1844, he told her:

> The home [*mone?*] has been for a time suspended on this ground: of all who wish to join it only one is actually free, two others could join it by being released from their engagements, but it seemed to be the wish of some who were interested in it, to wait until there should be two of independent means, and two of dependent. I expect an answer in time, but at present it seems that we must wait and pray for a Sisterhood.

On 18 September he wrote to Miss Ellacombe, counselling her at length:

> You must make up your mind to be disappointed: you will have an ideal of what things should be and find that the foundation only is being laid,

that everything is to be worked out step by step, that there is little apparent fruit, that the very rules are to be gradually framed, that people with right ends still have infirmities clinging to them, that feelings have such different modes of expression that you may not understand one another, that nothing will be in order, you will have to school yourself not to be impatient at "the day of small things", to bear all manner of crosses of what you think best, perhaps dreariness and dryness of heart, and all those trials by which God premits the perseverance of those to be tried who in some new and higher way would serve Him. Your first office will be with yourself; to tend towards perfection is your first object, to make yourself better—pleasing to Him whose Spouse you would be. Use all things to this end, and He will bless all.

The books which I was thinking of, are books on the spiritual life, on self-examination and on mental prayer. I thought of asking you whether you would like to assist in translating any so that any profits which there might ultimately be, might go towards the Institution. . . .

You ought to think also that the probable occupation of the Sisterhood in the first instance, will probably not be instruction, but visiting, this being the want which has most been felt by those who have set this plan on foot, though one hardly knows which evil is most crying. But I suppose teaching may ultimately be combined with it, or as it enlarges in time, by God's blessing it might branch off into different objects and each Sister take that most adapted to her. I say this because your own talents seem to lie towards teaching. . . . You say you do not know how to address me—as one who would help those younger, if he could.

A fresh stage in the preparations began with correspondence between Dr Pusey and Mr Dodsworth in the autumn. Dodsworth had had nearly twenty years of parochial experience and was a much more practical man than his academic correspondent. On the eve of St Michael (28 September) 1844 Dodsworth wrote:

Our lay friends agreed that they would find the means to open the house if *three* or *four* inmates approved by us offered themselves: these conditions I consider fulfilled as follows

1. Miss Moore
2. Miss Ellacombe
3. Miss Langston
4. The Governess, though the time is uncertain. . . .

From what you say I hope Miss Langston will prove competent for the office of Superior, and then one of our great difficulties will be surmounted; for then we may think of those who are to come in more as those to be *influenced*, than as to have influence.

In an undated fragment he pointed out:

> In considering the question of strictness we must remember that probably our best members will be satisfied with nothing short of a *very strict rule*, and that the place would lose its special recommendation *to them*, if much relaxation were allowed.

On 8 October Dr Pusey suggested to Mr Ellacombe that his daughter might live temporarily in lodgings in Keble's parish of Hursley, where another aspirant, Miss Moore, was already living. There "she could prepare herself . . . tranquilly for the life she hopes for. It will be no expense: your daughter will employ herself in the translations, in requital". In other words Dr Pusey would support her. This plan miscarried. In a letter of 27 October he told Mr Ellacombe:

> The state of Miss Moore's health has presented an unexpected hindrance, and you will have heard, I conclude, from Keble (from whom I have just heard finally) that he does not think that there can be any good arrangement for your daughter there at present.

Two other possibilities of residing in a suitable parish were discussed. "There might be yet another plan: instruction in a school for a time, carried on by two religious sisters, where she might have the benefits of counsel from Archdeacon Manning."

Two days later Dr Pusey explained that the school was one established at Chichester by Mrs Lockhart, the widow of a priest and the mother of another, and the step-mother of Miss Elizabeth Lockhart (who was eventually to be the first Mother of the Community established in Wantage by its new vicar, W. J. Butler, in 1848). One of the other teachers was Miss Mary Reid who was destined to be Miss Lockhart's first companion in the Wantage Sisterhood and was to follow her into the Roman Catholic Church in 1851. In November Miss Ellacombe wrote to Dr Pusey from Chichester that she was now in Mrs Lockhart's care and "no longer under her father, who had given her his blessing when she left home". She hoped that Dr Pusey would forgive her, if it seemed a very presumptuous request that he would accept from her the obedience of a child and would treat her as such—set her about what he would, and "blame and punish her mistakes—and not 'Miss Ellacombe' her any more", but permit her

The Reverend W. Dodsworth

The Reverend E. B. Pusey
from a pen-and-ink drawing of the 1830s

to call him "her dear father in Christ". She was "ready, with God's help, to render him an unquestioning obedience".

Preparations went on during the winter. Dr Pusey already had the assistance of Miss Marian Hughes. A physician, Dr Greenhill, obtained for him copies of the respective Rules of St Francis of Sales and of St Vincent de Paul. Lord John Manners procured the Rule of the Birmingham Sisters of Mercy. Dr Wiseman, then President of Oscott College, in a letter dated 18 January 1845, sent "the order of the day as set out for the Sisters of Mercy at Birmingham" with a note about their meditation and spiritual reading.

Dr Pusey's own account of the sources of the rule of the Sisterhood was given in a letter to Mr A. J. Beresford-Hope in 1848:

> We naturally went by experience. Lord John Manners procured us the Rule of the Sisters of Charity of Birmingham [a mistake for Sisters of Mercy]. I had some rules by me, used by different bodies in England and on the continent. We took as our basis St Augustine's Rule, as extant in an epistle of his to some "Sanctimoniales" whom he had brought together, thinking it most in accordance with our Church to take Rules from one of the Fathers of the Church. On this we engrafted others, always bearing in mind the character of English Churchwomen. When it was done, Dodsworth and myself looked over it, with a view to what the Bishop of London would think; and several little points were altered (language, chiefly) on his saying, "The Bishop would not like that". This was kept to be shown to the Bishop, whenever trial enough had been made of the institution thus for him to be ready to take it up. . . . When we had reviewed the rules, we showed them to John Keble.

In a letter to Miss Hughes dated Lent 1845 Dr Pusey said:

> You will be glad to know that the little Sisterhood is to enter upon its abode on Wednesday in Easter week. In the first instance there will be three only, but there are six more purposing to come, when engagements or health permit, so that before the close of this year I trust it will consist of eight or nine devoted persons. You will pray for it and they will specially pray for all who look to the same mode of life. It is very wonderful how persons, who like yourself have still domestic duties, are preparing themselves in earnest for this mode of life.
>
> I thank you very much for your kind offer to obtain information about details in the Convent life. One thing which I most wished to learn is *the distribution of time*, especially in the afternoon, for in their books I find what is done at the beginning of an hour, but not whether it lasts

c

to the end. Especially I should like to know exactly the employment of time given to devotion, wherein it is employed and how long. The most minute description of a Convent day—in every half or quarter of an hour—would be of most value to me. I have been especially puzzled as to the devotions in the latter part of each day.

2. I should much like to know wherein recreation consists. One of our Sisters seems puzzled. For it seems essential to keep out of mind the excitements and news of the world around them, to which they are dead. Is it then employed in spiritual conversation? This too is difficult for reserved persons. Or again does it become working and reading?

It is clear from this that Dr Pusey was as vague about the life of contemporary Roman Catholic convents as he was determined to use them as a model for the new Sisterhood.

The final plans were adjusted in correspondence between Dr Pusey and Mr Dodsworth. On 20 February 1845 Dodsworth wrote:

Do you think that under the existing circumstances of the Church it would be better to have the *general* rules separate from those which are to regulate the interior of the Home? The former might be shewn, but people have no business to enquire how the Sisters regulate their dress or diet—or their devotions, etc. Entire secrecy would expose us to suspicion and yet the publication of *all* our Rules would be inexpedient.

I quite agree with you that Confession should not be *required*, but I suppose it will be practised. At first as you say there will be no difficulty, but I have reason to think that there might be afterwards when the Sisterhood may become more numerous. We must remember that the sort of life will be quite new to them and that there may be some who may unconsciously mix up other feelings with the higher feelings.

In an undated letter, Mr Dodsworth suggested the use of the *Day Hours of the Church* published in English by the Reverend Albany Christie, who was to submit to the Church of Rome later in the year. "I suppose they might be used without any exception being taken to them."

About the middle of March Miss Ellacombe came up to London for medical advice from Dr Crawford. She was told to give up the Lenten fast. On Easter Monday, 24 March, Dr Pusey wrote to her father to reassure him. He took the opportunity to remind him:

You will kindly not forget that you gave your free consent to your daughter's going and your blessing with her, and told me that you did so as being, under the *circumstances*, the best thing. You also mentioned to me your wish that she should leave home as a governess, since having given up her marriage, she ought to provide for herself.

It is evident from the tone and purport of this letter that Mr Ellacombe was to the last wavering in his attitude towards his daughter's becoming a Sister of Mercy. Dr Pusey wrote on the Monday in Easter Week. Two days later, on the Wednesday of that week, 26 March 1845, Miss Ellacombe and another aspirant went into residence as Sisters of Mercy at No. 17 Park Village West, Upper Albany Street, Regent's Park.

APPENDED NOTE TO CHAPTER ONE

THE ROLE OF LUCY PUSEY
IN THE REVIVAL OF THE RELIGIOUS LIFE
IN THE ENGLISH CHURCH

In a letter to Canon Liddon, Mrs Hungerford, a daughter of the Reverend Edward R. Richards of Farlington, Hants, and sister of Charlotte and Mary Richards, who became Sisters of the Devonport Society, noted that Dr Pusey's elder daughter, Lucy Maria, and her own cousin, Helen Richards, "were almost the first young girls who thought of dedicating themselves as Sisters of Mercy". Of Helen Richards, Dr Pusey wrote to her uncle in 1845, that "he must ever regard her with deep interest as Lucy's first friend". It was through Helen Richards that her cousin Charlotte came to know of and to desire the Religious Life, which she embraced in 1850. Lucy Pusey's influence was not confined to girls of her own age. It was to association with her that Miss Etheldreda Benett, Foundress of the Society of the Sisters of Bethany, and Miss Mary Bruce, one of the two first Sisters of the Park Village Community, owed their knowledge of the Religious Life and the inspiration to give themselves to God in Holy Religion.

In a sermon preached in the Priory Church of Jesus Christ at Ascot on 15 September 1962, at the High Mass commemorating the eightieth anniversary of Dr Pusey's death, the Reverend Augustine Hoey of the Community of the Resurrection dwelt at length on the hidden but tremendously effective part played by Lucy Pusey, both before and after her death, in the revival of conventual life in the English Church, acclaiming her the "real Mother Foundress" of the

Park Village Community. The following extracts from Father Hoey's sermon are given by the kind permission of the preacher and his Superiors:

> What miracles God can work through a child! "A little child shall lead them", wrote Isaiah. Little did the prophet know, as we know now, how God would spark those words into life—St Joan of Arc, Bernardette of Lourdes, Thérèse of Lisieux, Lucy Maria Pusey, all adding their witness to St Paul's words, "God hath chosen the weak things of the world to confound the things which are mighty". In the cases of Thérèse of Lisieux and Lucy Maria of Oxford, the so-called wisdom of the world is even more confounded, for it was not until after their deaths that the full impact of their lives was felt. May we not paraphrase the passage from the Wisdom of Solomon appointed for the Epistle of the Feast of a Martyr in Eastertide, thus?—"We fools counted their life madness and their end to be without honour: but on the contrary how are they numbered among the children of God and their lot is among the Saints." We should not be surprised, for our Lord himself promised, "Except a corn of wheat fall into the ground and die, it abideth alone; but if it die, it bringeth forth much fruit". Lucy's father, at her death-bed, instead of reflecting, as we might, that his hopes for Religious Sisterhoods seemed destined to fail, for this daughter of his was to have been the chief-cornerstone, with victorious faith and knowing that God's ways are not as our ways, makes bold to say to her: "Pray for us all in the presence of the Redeemer, and if it might be, for those institutions to which you yourself hoped to belong." So did father and daughter co-operate in their restoration, and as the prayer of a righteous man availeth much, so the pleading of this virginal soul was so acceptable to God, that even before her body was laid to rest in Oxford, the first practical steps were taken at a meeting held in London for the foundation of the Sisterhood in Park Village West.
>
> We read that, like Thérèse of Lisieux, Lucy Maria longed to die a martyr. But theirs was to be only the martyrdom of intense illness, which early opened the gates of Paradise for them. Both were passionately devoted to the early Roman Virgin Martyrs, so that when Lucy lay dying and discussing with her father the design of the chalice she was giving—bought by a legacy left to her—to the famous Church of St Saviour which he was building in Leeds, she stipulated that of the four Saints to be engraved round the base, one should be our Lady, but the other three, the Virgin Martyrs, Agnes, Lucy, and Catharine.
>
> There are some who accomplish in a short time what others take long years to do. We are bewildered at the passionate pleading of Thérèse of Lisieux at the age of twelve to be a Carmelite nun, who although so

young had the faith that every obstacle could be removed, and so perse-
vered, even to speaking to the Pope himself, that at fifteen she was in
Carmel. It is the kind of thing we can compare with Lucy, who at the
age of twelve was taken, as a source of inspiration, to visit some of the
Irish convents by her father. She witnessed at the clothing of Novices
the exchange of the glittering bridal gowns for the black serge, and on
being asked which dress she preferred, said, "The black". Of her death
her father wrote to her brother, Philip; "All at once her eyes opened
wide and I never saw such a gaze at what was invisible to us, which continued for some time; and after this had continued for some little while,
she looked me full in the face and there came such an unearthly smile,
so full of love also, all expression of pain disappeared and was swallowed
up in joy: I never saw anything like that smile; there was no sound, else
it seemed almost a laugh for joy and I could hardly help laughing for joy
in answer. I cannot describe it, it was utterly unlike anything I ever saw,
it seemed as if she would say, 'All you have longed for me is fulfilled',
and when her blessed spirit was gone her eyes which were looking
heavenwards retained such lustre that they seemed more than living. It
turned at once all sorrow into joy, it seemed like one in Paradise in-
viting me thither. . . . I feel certain that it was our Blessed Lord whom
she saw: I had often in the night used part of that prayer, 'Soul of Christ
sanctify me . . .' more than once as a whole and especially that part, 'O
good Jesu hear me' and 'Suffer me not to be separated from Thee'.
I repeated to her the blessing, 'May the face of our Lord Jesus Christ
appear to thee mild and joyous'. The lustre of her eyes and the heavenly
love of the smile seemed a reflection of His Countenance."

It has been suggested, with great plausibility, that Dr Pusey's
devotion and avowedly paternal affection towards Mother Priscilla
Lydia Sellon (so cruelly misinterpreted by the enemies of both and
misunderstood by their friends) was grounded primarily on the
realization in Mother Lydia of the hopes and aspirations which he
had entertained for Lucy as the destined "restorer after three centuries
of the Religious Life in the English Church".

2

The First Sisters
1845

"The house for this first Anglican Sisterhood" is described in a letter of Miss Marian Hughes quoted in Miss Trench's *Story of Dr Pusey's Life:* "No 17 Park Village West was not like a London house; it had a pretty garden round it, and looked like one of the very tiny villas one sees in the environs of London." The house, which survived the heavy bombing of the district during the Second World War,[1] was built by John Nash, the architect of the Terraces in Regent's Park and of other less pretentious dwellings in the same district, on land leased from the Commissioners of Crown Lands. Park Village West is a collection of villa-like dwellings "built around a 'serpentine' road, approached from Albany Street" immediately opposite what was in 1845 the Precinct of the Royal Hospital of St Katherine.[2]

[1] In her letter to Miss Trench Miss Hughes stated that "the house has long since been swept away for a more regular street" (*The Story of Dr Pusey's Life*, p. 268). This erroneous statement was perpetuated in *Priscilla Lydia Sellon* (p. 20), but is here corrected on the authority of the present occupant of No. 17 Park Village West, Dr Janet Niven, through whose kindness it has been possible to include among the illustrations of the present work the photograph of the house. Dr Niven also supplied information concerning the house before 1845.

[2] Mr Peter F. Anson, in the second edition of *The Call of the Cloister* (p. 27) pertinently remarks: "It is curious that neither Robert Southey nor anybody else in the eighteen twenties who felt the need of Protestant Sisters of Charity appears to have realized that the nucleus of one such community had existed in the Church of England since the Reformation—the *Royal Foundation of St Katherine*. Founded by Queen Matilda in 1148, and refounded by Queen Eleanor in 1273, this community, which, according to its statutes, consisted of a Master and three Brethren in Holy Orders, and three Sisters of equal rank, had managed to weather the religious upheaval of the sixteenth century. The *Book of Common Prayer* took the place of whatever office was recited during the first four centuries of its existence, but the works of charity and mercy carried on remained much the same." When in 1826 the original site of the Hospital, near the Tower of London, was needed for St Katherine's Docks, "the community moved to new buildings [in] Regent's Park, designed in the 'Gothick' style by Ambrose

Christ Church, which was to be the Sisters' spiritual home, stands on the same side of Albany Street as Park Village West, at some ten minutes' distance to the south. The relative proximity of Park Village West to the church and the avowed sympathy of its incumbent with the proposal to establish a Sisterhood of Mercy in the Church of England were determining factors in the choice by the Committee of Laymen of No. 17 Park Village West as the home of the Sisterhood. The house was taken on sub-lease by the Committee in the name of Lord John Manners.

The interior of the house is described in detail in the reminiscences which one of the Sisters of early days compiled for the use of Canon Liddon in his account of the Sisterhood in the third volume of *The Life of E. B. Pusey*. The house contained on the ground floor "an Oratory, Recreation Room, and Parlour, leading into each other. The upper rooms were partitioned into six small cells and there were four attics. The kitchen served as Refectory. All were plainly furnished. The Oratory had a small altar table with a black cross and scarlet cover, a few little prayer-desks down each side, two benches, and a lamp. [There was] also a picture of the Crucifixion in one corner from Albrecht Dürer by Mrs Dodsworth. The walls and windows were hung with red baize." The furnishing of the Sisters' cells is described by Mr Dodsworth in a letter addressed to Dr Pusey on Saturday in Mid-Lent, 1845, as consisting of an iron bedstead, with coarse sheets, a straw mattress, a flock bolster, a wash-stand, a closet with shelves to be used as a clothes-press, a chair and table, some shelves for books, and a "lock-up place" for papers.

Dr Pusey wrote to Mr Keble on 1 March announcing the date set for the opening of the house as some time in Easter Week. The

---

Poynter". Equally remarkable is the fact that the house chosen for the home of the Sisterhood designed to be a memorial of Southey in fulfilment of his wish that there might be "Sisters of Charity" in the Church of England, should have been situated within sight and walking distance of this single and singular survival in that Church of medieval communal life where the "Sisters" of the Foundation carried on a school for poor children and undertook the care of ten poor "bedeswomen"—two of the works of mercy which the projected Sisterhood was expected to undertake. Nor is there any evidence that the incumbent of Christ Church or his coadjutors in the establishment of the Sisterhood of Mercy were aware of the semi-monastic character of the neighbouring institution. It should be noted that the incumbent of Christ Church had no pastoral jurisdiction or responsibility in relation to this institution within his district, in as much as the Foundation was a "Royal Peculiar", exempt from both episcopal and parochial control.

actual day was 26 March 1845, the Wednesday after Easter, when the two first aspirants arrived to take up their residence in Park Village West. One was Miss Jane Ellacombe, the other was Miss Mary Bruce, a lady of Scottish ancestry and Irish birth, who had been known to Dr Pusey for some time.[1] Miss Ellacombe was twenty-six years old. Miss Bruce was thirty-two.

Two days after their arrival Dr Pusey wrote to Mr Keble (28 March):

> Two Sisters entered their home on Easter Wednesday, one Miss E[llacombe]. They are very promising; a third we expect on Friday week. . . . Dodsworth and myself had a little service with them on Wednesday; they were in floods of tears, but of joy, in the prayers for them. On Sunday, March 30, at a quarter to eight is to be their first Communion subsequent to their solemn entrance . . . . There are no vows, but they have given themselves for life.

The third aspirant expected by Dr Pusey was Miss Sarah Anne Terrot, a daughter of the Right Reverend Charles Hughes Terrot, D.D., Bishop of Edinburgh, 1841–72. Miss Terrot "had a regard and reverence for Dr Pusey from a long letter he wrote in 1838 to the Bishop of Oxford".[2] During the winter of 1844–5, her father wrote to Dr Pusey that, although he was "very far from those tendencies which commonly went by the name of Tractarian, two of his daughters had 'a desire for greater usefulness and for more intimate communion with persons whom they could look to as real followers of Christ' than was afforded by their native Scotland. . . . So the Bishop, 'despairing of their viewing their present position more favourably', gave 'not a reluctant consent' to their wish to join a Sisterhood".[3] Only one of the Bishop's daughters, however, was ready to join the Community when the time of action came. The

---

[1] Lucy Pusey, during her last illness in 1844, in choosing jewels for adorning the chalice which she was presenting to her father's votive church of St Saviour's, Leeds, wished to include both rubies and carbuncles. Miss Bruce is said to have given for the purpose a set of carbuncles "which had been her mother's". This would indicate that Miss Bruce was acquainted with Dr Pusey as early as 1844. It is not impossible or improbable that the acquaintance began when Dr Pusey and Lucy visited Ireland in 1841. That Miss Bruce lived in Scotland prior to her coming to Park Village West is implied in a memorandum at Ascot Priory to the effect that when she left Oxford in 1854 she "returned" to Scotland.

[2] The letter referred to is quoted in its original form, as written in 1837, in Liddon's *Life of E. B. Pusey*, Vol. II, pp. 14–17. Miss Terrot's reference is to the expanded form in which the letter was published in 1838.

[3] The Bishop's letter was accompanied by a note from Mrs Terrot of like tenor.

younger Miss Terrot, Catherine, was said to be held back by "Roman-izing tendencies". Her sister, who did come to Park Village West, Sarah Anne Terrot, was twenty-five years old when she entered the Sisterhood. "I went by steamer", she wrote in later years to Miss Trench, "arriving at 17 Park Village West on April 4. Dr Pusey came soon after and prayed with us and had Compline".

A week later (April 11) Sister Jane Ellacombe wrote to her father, describing the external life of herself and her companions:

.... I am now, thank God, getting very well and strong again, and we are happy—we three. Our district is in the worst part of Mr Dodsworth's district—where there are a great many low Irish people. They give away a great deal here to the poor, but there is such a great deal of misery and excessive poverty amongst our people. I call that our district, for it has no other regular visitors than the clergy, but wherever there is any distress made known to us we are to go, though while [we are] few Fitzroy Place will suffice us, I think, for some time. The people are all very glad and thankful for our coming to them—and we have not met with anything like a word of rudeness. We go to them to relieve their bodily wants, but principally our office lies in religious instruction and guidance.... We do not find (though you will say that we have not had long trial) that we have too long a time for visiting; it is about a quarter of an hour's walk from home, besides which we have plenty of exercise going up and down stairs to the different floors. We are out from nine till one, and again after dinner from a little after three till five. The recreation hours are from a quarter after two till three, and from seven till eight.... Mr Dodsworth is very kind. He orders all about our visiting; we do not know anyone else but Mrs Dodsworth and one lady, beside Dr Crawford.

The letter concludes with a request for her copy of Pearson *On the Creed*, which was not to be directed to her by name, "but only 17 Park Village West. Everything of that sort is common property and of course", she added, "we are no longer known as Miss This or Miss That[1].... We live in a very quiet place; the house does not join any other; and there is very little passing".

[1] In a letter to Dr Pusey, dated "before Passion Sunday, 1845", Mr Dodsworth raised the question of "more suitable names" for some of the Sisters—Sister Jane, specifically—than their Christian names. Dr Pusey was in favour of their retaining their baptismal names, but gave rather reluctant consent to Miss Ellacombe's being known in the Community as "Sister Anne". By this name she is referred to in Mr Dodsworth's letters. In a letter to her sister, dated 21 September 1848, the some-time Sister Anne signed herself "Sister Jane". When Miss Cusack joined the Sisterhood in 1850, Miss

It was not until May that Miss Emma Langston, the lady chosen
for the office of Superior, arrived at No. 17 Park Village West. A
native of the City of London, Miss Langston, to be known in Religion
as Mother Emma, was forty-one years old, ten years older than any
of the other Sisters. Her family were Cheshire folk from Altrincham.
She was introduced to Dr Pusey by the Reverend James Isaacson in
July 1844 as "a person of strong understanding, fervent piety, and
extreme simplicity of manners . . . well fitted to make one of the
charitable Sisters so much needed in our Church". At the time when
Mr Isaacson wrote, Miss Langston was residing at Bassingham, near
Newark. When she wrote to Dr Pusey on 26 July following she was
in Ireland, at Claremont, Bray, near Dublin, where she was engaged
as governess of the daughters of a Mr Quin. Unwillingness to cause
inconvenience to her employers by asking for an early release from
her engagement delayed her joining the Sisters at Park Village West
until the following June, 1845. Before entering on her duties she
informed both Dr Pusey and Mr Dodsworth that she had never
been confirmed. "I suppose this is from having lacked opportunity."
Mr Dodsworth wrote to Dr Pusey on 28 April 1845. "It seems to be
inverting the order of things", he added, "to aim at a high life, while
labouring under such a serious disqualification".[1] To remedy this
omission, Mr Dodsworth undertook to arrange for Miss Langston's
confirmation at one of the later Episcopal Visitations of the season.
He hoped that she would think her confirmation of sufficient importance to justify her hastening her coming to London, as "he did not
think [the Sisterhood] would go on quite satisfactorily until they had
a Superior".

Those who knew Mother Emma have described her as "a lady of

Ellacombe was known as Sister Jane. Miss Terrot, known at first by her first name
Sarah, was known in 1850 as Sister Anne. As a member of the Devonport Society, she
was known as Sister (or Eldress) Sarah Anne. In the present work, except in quotations,
Miss Ellacombe is referred to as Sister Jane.

[1] What Mr Dodsworth rightly considered "a serious disqualification" was not un-
common, even in the case of devout churchmen and regular communicants in the years
preceding the Tractarian Revival. A pertinent case, not unlike Miss Langston's, was
that of Mrs Louisa Taylor, mother of the Eldress Phoebe of the Devonport Society,
and of Mother Magdalene Taylor, foundress of the Poor Servants of the Mother of
God. Mrs Taylor was the wife of the Reverend Henry Taylor, for many years incumbent of a church in Lincolnshire, and a devout churchwoman, yet she was not confirmed
until 1853, when she was nearly sixty years old, "not before this time being convinced
that at any age it is advisable to avail [oneself] of such a privilege."—F. C. Devas,
s. J., *Mother Magdalene Taylor* (New York 1927), pp. 80–1.

great refinement and goodness, whose very countenance indicated benevolence". She was endowed with "considerable culture", being acquainted with Latin and French. "Kind, motherly and gentle" are the adjectives used by one of the Sisters who knew her well. Dr Pusey through his correspondence with her had been "impressed by her fervent desire to engage in a more devoted service to God and in works destined to relieve the poor and afflicted, and still more by the anxious self-distrust . . . apparent in her correspondence". Writing to the Reverend Mr Ellacombe shortly after Miss Langston came to Park Village West, he characterized her as "a very thoughtful, superior, quiet person . . . just the motherly person one would wish; a very religious, devoted person of mature age, very tender, gentle and considerate, who loved and valued the Sisters very much and they her".

The difficulties which Mother Emma encountered were "immense", due to the "entire inexperience, both in the leaders and those who had to be led. . . . She could not give training which she had never received herself". Such knowledge as she eventually acquired of the duties of a Superior, as of every other phase of the Religious Life, were theoretical, derived at second hand from the study of published conventual Rules and of such treatises on the Religious Life as *Les Entrétiens* of St François de Sales and the ascetic works of St Alphonsus Liguori, from the instructions of Dr Pusey, or from suggestions of Miss Hughes based on first-hand observation of conventual life in France.[1]

With all her inexperience, Mother Emma was most conscientious in the fulfilment of every duty as a Religious and as a Superior, so far as she understood them, setting an example to the other Sisters of hard work, unflagging devotion, and real love of the poor. Being naturally of a strong constitution she "never spared herself: she worked harder than anyone else". These excellent and endearing qualities could not, however, make up for her lack of "that decision of character so eminently necessary for successful government". The "anxious self-distrust" which at first had impressed Dr Pusey as a sign of Miss Langston's genuine humility, he came in time to recognize as an estimate of her own limitations which he would have done well to heed.

[1] Miss Langston told a former novice, Miss Cusack, that she had long been familiar with the Rule of the Visitation Nuns "in the original French". ([Cusack], *Five Years*, p. 30).

The experiment in Regent's Park was saved from utter failure by the union of the Sisterhood of the Holy Cross with a Society whose Superior (with even less training and no more experience than Mother Emma) had the advantages of youthful enthusiasm, broad vision, indomitable will, and those innate qualities of leadership which Miss Langston lacked. It was only after several years that Dr Pusey came to realize, as he wrote twenty years later to the Reverend A. H. Stanton, that "when the Superior is unfit for her office . . . (as I have seen at [Park Village West]), it would be better to delay the existence of the Society until God should give a fit Superior".

During the formative years of the Regent's Park Community, the one woman in the English Church fitted for the office of Foundress and Superior was hindered by the dependence of her mother from embracing Community Life. But as in the establishment of the Sisterhood and the drafting of its Rule, Miss Hughes had put at Dr Pusey's service the fruits of her experience of conventual life on the Continent, so she was of great help to him in his exercise of those duties of a Superior which Mother Emma was not qualified to discharge.

The fulfilment of his two-fold responsibility of Spiritual Superintendent and virtual Superior of the new Community made it necessary for Dr Pusey "to spend the greater part of each day", whenever he was in London, "at the Sisterhood . . . from early morning until eight or nine at night". A Novice, who left the Community before Profession, stated in her account of *Five Years in a Protestant Sisterhood* that when Dr Pusey "came to hear confessions . . . he always went into the sacristy and remained there the greater part of the day. Each Sister went to him in regular rotation and he never left the apartment, except for the brief interval occupied in taking some refreshment". The Sister whose reminiscences supplied Canon Liddon with information concerning the Sisterhood, stated that Dr Pusey "never took a solid meal in the Home. He never ate with anyone. The Sisters provided him with milk and coffee, and this with a morsel of dry bread was all he took during his visits".

The same Sister relates that "after the coming of the kind, loving and gentle . . . Superior, the numbers quickly increased". On 30 August Dr Pusey, in reply to a letter from Mr Keble expressing the wish "that he could hear of the number of Sisters increasing", wrote that "God was giving the increase . . . the number of Sisters (four) was to be doubled by Christmas". The fifth, he added, "had come that day, strongly recommended by Dr Mill,[1] a very interesting person, aged twenty-two". Five days later (3 September) Mr Dodsworth wrote to Dr Pusey: "In your next tell me what you think of Sister Etheldreda." Dr Pusey's reply has not been found. But his estimate of Sister Etheldreda as expressed in a letter to Dr Mill written at this time is indicated by Dr Mill's reply, dated at Brasted, 13 September 1845.

> I am truly obliged by your very kind and cheering letter [he wrote]. It is most gratifying to find such a confirmation of the view I had taken of the spiritual character of my young friend, and most thankful am I to hear of the affectionate sympathy with which she has been received, and the happy prospect before her of realizing the life she so evidently desired. I trust that in this we may indeed see in this and other similar instances a token of Christ's presence being yet with us, notwithstanding the distressing and alarming symptoms of the times, and that better things are yet reserved for our Church, though some of our best friends seem to despair of her.

Of Sister Etheldreda the ex-novice Margaret Anna Cusack wrote in her *Story of my Life*: "Sister Etheldreda . . . was certainly a lady, a bright, gay . . . bit of sunshine in the house . . . It was whispered that she helped 'Father', as Dr Pusey was called, in his translations." Miss Hughes, recording in her diary a visit to the Sisterhood in September 1848, made special mention of Sister Etheldreda, who she "thought charming". Miss Cusack "never knew exactly who her family were". They have recently been identified. Sister Etheldreda was a grand-daughter of William Gooch Pillans of Bracondale, Norfolk, a gentleman of Scottish descent. She had been brought up by her father's sister, Amelia, Lady Ward, widow of the late Reverend William Ward, tenth Baron Ward of Birmingham and Rector of the family living of Himley, Wolverhampton. Sister Etheldreda was one of those who "made the three vows" on admission to the Sisterhood. It was said of her by one who knew her: "Jesus was her first and only Love."

The sixth Sister arrived not long after Miss Pillans. She was the

[1] Dr William Hodge Mill, sometime Principal of Bishop's College, Calcutta (1820–38); Chaplain to the Archbishop of Canterbury (Howley, 1838); Hulsean Advocate (1839), and Regius Professor of Hebrew, Cambridge (1848–53). From 1843 to 1853 Dr Mill was incumbent of Brasted, Kent.

youngest daughter of a Scottish laird, John Hamilton Colt, late of Gartsherrie, near Coatbridge in Lanarkshire. Caroline Augusta Colt, to be known in Religion as Sister Caroline,[1] was one of the "seven from Edinburgh" who aspired to the Religious Life as early as 1844. Mr Dodsworth had been for some time in correspondence with Miss Colt and her parish priest, the Reverend John Alexander, at that time incumbent of Old St Paul's, Edinburgh, and later founder of St Columba's-by-the-Castle, the outpost of Tractarianism in Scotland. Mr Alexander wished to establish a parochial Sisterhood on non-conventual lines, and urged Miss Colt to join in the enterprise. Dr Pusey became interested in the case of Miss Colt through Mr Dodsworth and seems to have written to her, advising her to join the Sisterhood being formed in London. The part played by Dr Pusey in bringing her to the decision to do so and her coming to Park Village West in September in consequence of his advice, so incensed Mr Alexander "that he put into the fire unread a letter which Dr Pusey wrote to soften his displeasure".

Of Sister Jane Mr Dodsworth wrote to Dr Pusey early in December, some six months after her coming into the Sisterhood: "[She] has the ideal of the life of a nun. All about her seems to be *everything* one could wish." The Miss Terrot who did not come to Park Village West was more drawn to the Sisterhood by the "desire to live as a nun" than her sister, Sarah Anne, who did come. Known as Sister Sarah as long as Miss Ellacombe was known as Sister Anne, Miss Terrot did not share her sister's desire for the life of a nun. Naturally shy, and self-distrustful to a fault, devoted to the poor who "loved her as a mother", "capable and trustworthy", "she did not like the life" of a Religious. She would have preferred, it was said, to "take service as a housemaid". In speech "unmistakably Scotch" [*sic*], of medium height, she was "possessed of remarkable strength", which on one occasion enabled her to "lift a man of more than ordinary size and height from the ground and set him on his feet" when he fainted from hunger in the street, and on another occasion to carry a fainting novice "down a long refectory, through a stone corridor, and . . . up a long, high flight of stairs".

[1] There were three ladies named Caroline—two of them Caroline Augusta—among the members or aspirants of the Park Village Community: Caroline Augusta Colt (1845–7); Caroline Paul (1851); and Caroline Augusta Madox (later Blackwood), who was at an early date associated with the Regent's Park Sisterhood and eventually became a Sister of the Devonport Society, as related below.

Ardent and sincere in their desire to dedicate themselves to God and the service of the poor in the Religious Life, these women came to the Sisterhood with ill-formed and often romantic conceptions of that life—whether it were Sister Jane's "ideal of the life of a nun" or Sister Sarah Terrot's concept of consecrated philanthropy. The youngest was twenty-two years old. The ages of the others ranged from twenty-three to forty-one. Their habits of thought and action had been moulded by domestic and social traditions alien to the Catholic ideal of Religious Vocation. Mr Dodsworth was not unaware, as he wrote to Dr Pusey on 28 November, of the danger of sentimental attachment to their spiritual guides on the part of young women "brought", as these Sisters were, "from spheres such as theirs had been and finding themselves at once the objects of devoted service from such as Dr Pusey". Sister Jane's "ideal of the life of a nun", which two months earlier had given Mr Dodsworth evident satisfaction, was now causing him considerable apprehension; for he added to the warning note cited above: "That they *think* of themselves 'very much as nuns' I never doubted; this is what I regret to see. I wish they could think less of what they *seem* to be, and let this gradually grow out of the reality. I do not mean that there is more than we might naturally expect of this tendency, but surely it is wise to repress it, and lead them to think little of themselves and their ways."

Mr Keble shared Mr Dodsworth's apprehensions. "It strikes me," he wrote to Dr Pusey, on 28 August, "that there is a particular danger incident to persons situated as those Sisters are among us, namely, that being so very few and among persons so deeply interested for them and their undertaking, they may very easily think too much of themselves, and be made too much of, and I could fancy that it might be necessary to do some violence to ourselves in order not to flatter them unconsciously."

Had Miss Hughes been free in 1845 to join Miss Ellacombe, Miss Bruce, and Miss Terrot and the other women who soon followed them in the first steps towards the revival of the Religious Life, the acquaintance with conventual life which she had gained during her visits to Norman convents in 1841 would have enabled her to save the Sisterhood from the errors, due to inexperience, which marked and marred the early stages of the experiment. It was Miss Hughes herself, who after several months' residence in Park Village West, noted in her diary a lack of naturalness and ease in the fledgeling English Sisters, which was in striking contrast to the "repose of the French nuns". She found the Sisters in Regent's Park "very good and earnest"; but she missed the "tone" which "the long years of life in an old Order gave to ... the foreign convent". The Park Village Sisters were "loving and devout, but learning their life, not sure as to minute usages, which gave them a coldness and stiffness of manner".[1] While Miss Hughes was "grateful for the love around her", the atmosphere of constraint "made her less at home than she had been with the Ursulines in Bayeux".

When Dr Pusey wrote to Miss Hughes in September 1845, not long after the coming of Miss Pillans and Miss Colt, he was filled with happy anticipation and hope for the future:

> With regard to the little Sisterhood, it is growing in numbers, and they in the grace of God. It is one of the brightest spots I know of. The Superior is a most admirable person, and one of the Sisters (a most beautiful, child-like, devotional mind of no ordinary caste) has quite the ideal of a convent life. [2] I do hope that this is the blossom of rich fruit. The Sisters are only in their external work under the superintendence of Mr D[odsworth][3] .... The house, which is a small one, only holding ten, will probably soon overflow. .... The little Sisterhood is feeling its way, or rather being led on of God.

[1] Writing to Miss Hughes (then Mother Marian) in 1890 concerning the visit referred to above, Sister Clara Powell asked the Mother if she "recollected [Sister Clara's] taking her to the dentist and being so very strict" (stiff in manner?). It was this "strictness" which no doubt was one reason why Sister Sarah Anne Terrot "did not like the life" and hoped to find a different "tone" in the Devonport Society when she joined it in 1849. It is certainly one cause, at least, of another's decision, after a visit to Park Village West "to see what a Sisterhood was like", "not to join the Community at Park Village, but to form another, of which she should herself be Superior".

[2] The Sister referred to was almost certainly Sister Jane Ellacombe (known at the time as Sister Anne), of whom Mr Dodsworth wrote to Dr Pusey in December 1845, that she "had more of the ideal of [a nun] than the rest".

[3] When the district of Christ Church, Albany Street, was chosen as the future scene of the ministrations of the projected Sisterhood of Mercy, it was with the expectation that the incumbent, Mr Dodsworth would be the spiritual guide—the pastor—of the Sisters. After a time—in 1844, when plans were being made for the ordering of the life of the Sisters—Mr Dodsworth became aware of Dr Pusey's greater knowledge of the principles of the Religious Life as compared to his own, and in a letter written at the time, of which only a fragment remains, he wrote to Dr. Pusey: "The more I think of the matter, I fear I have undertaken a task which I am unequal to and unfitted for. In all the interior work you must consider me only as being on the spot your assistant." This became the recognized arrangement. Dr Pusey, Sister Clara wrote in her Reminiscences, "was considered as the Founder, and his office was that of Spiritual

The Right Reverend A. P. Forbes
Bishop of Brechin, in 1850

The Right Reverend C. J. Blomfield
Bishop of London

Christ Church, Albany Street

Mr Dodsworth had written to Dr Pusey as early as the Lent of 1845, when details of the Rule and other matters concerning the ordering of the Community were being discussed, of the necessity of restraining the Sisters from "over fasting", lest they should soon have "a house of invalids". By October of that year this state of affairs was well on the way to being realized. Of a Community of seven women there were three "little able to work". The health of Sister Jane, Sister Mary, and Sister Caroline had given way, putting an end to their external work. "Sister Mary . . . soon required all the attention that could be given her." Sister Jane's activities were limited to prayer and the church needle-work in which she excelled. Sister Caroline, soon after her coming, developed symptoms which Dr Crawford, the Sisters' physician, thought to be "decidedly consumptive", although as yet there was "no actual disease". As a preventive measure he suggested that the patient be "shut up in an atmosphere of seventy", lest "if she caught a bad cold, she should go off in a decline". In addition to her consumptive tendency, Sister Caroline "had a stomach complaint" which a physician of the present day would no doubt diagnose as ulcers, due to the "extreme nervous sensitiveness" noted by Mr Dodsworth, and to other emotional tensions. Dr Crawford forbade her to fast. This "tried her greatly" —adding another tension.

When Mr Dodsworth wrote to Dr Pusey on 3 September, the number of Sisters had increased to seven. The seventh Sister, Miss Elizabeth Wilcox,[1] had been received into the Community between the coming of Miss Colt in September and a letter written by Mr Dodsworth on 23 or 25 November, in which he attributed "to some indiscretion in Sister Elizabeth, especially in the absence of a due reserve", the alarm among the poor of the congregation in regard to the Sisters. "Their usefulness", he wrote, "was greatly threatened", in consequence of the poor "regarding them with suspicion instead of love and veneration" as heretofore. This "revulsion of feeling" was partly due to the suspicion, fostered by the recent secessions to Rome among the Tractarians, that the Sisters were "disguised Roman

---

Superintendent". She noted, however, that two of the Sisters who had been introduced to the Community by Mr Dodsworth were "his spiritual children" and that another was under the guidance of Mr Upton Richards and another under the direction of an unnamed priest. The rest "had the privilege of having Dr Pusey for their spiritual father".

[1] A remark in a letter of Mr Upton Richards suggests that she may have been one of the ladies "introduced" by him.

D

Catholics". Mr Dodsworth "did not think that these alarms . . . origi-
nated with the poor". Rather, "alas! there were plenty of emissaries—
dissenters and others—who would be too glad to excite suspicion".
Earlier in the month there had been "a falling off in . . . attendance"
of the poor, which Mr Dodsworth had attributed to certain "alterations in the church" which might be interpreted as indicating "a tendency to Romanism". This falling off "had recently become still
more marked".

Mr Dodsworth, attributing the hostility towards the Sisters in part
to prejudice against their "peculiar dress", thought that it would be
advisable for two or three of them to wear "a more ordinary dress
out of doors, such as black and white or coloured shawls . . . which
would break the uniformity, which our people are unused to". He
did not think it well to let "the poor know that any change was
adopted for the sake of conciliation". While "he would not have one
essential point given up", he urged the desirability of all they could
to "soften prejudices". He added: "Nothing has ever been *simply
restored*, so we can never have nuns again, though we may have something resembling them." Dr Pusey was not in favour of compromise.
The most he would assent to was a slight alteration of the Sisters'
habit, consisting of the "introduction of a little white about the neck",
which, he said, Mother Emma was sure "would make a difference".
This slight change, and "dividing them in their walk" to and from
church, succeeded in making the Sisters less conspicuous, and saved
them from attracting attention.

Sister Elizabeth, whose want of reserve had contributed to the
feeling against the Sisters, left the Community before Christmas.
The excitement and revulsion died down as the people of the district
learned by experience the true character of the Sisters. Some time
later Dr Pusey was able to relate an incident which showed how much
the Sisters were loved. "An arch of the house gave way. No harm
happened: the house was propped up. But in their district the report
was that 'the house had given way and they must all have been killed
but that they were such good people'. But indeed one hears abundantly
how much they are beloved. . . . A poor woman said of one of them,
'She came to me like an angel sent from God'. Soon after that," Dr
Pusey added, "they visited in a street where I understand that no
ladies visited, and were well received." The poor people soon came
to know that "those who came to their houses came, not out of

curiosity, to spy out their wretchedness, but for the love of God. ...
At the beginning of their visiting two [of the Sisters] went into one
of the brothels" in the district. "Even there they were let go without
rudeness."

The eighth Sister whom Dr Pusey expected before Christmas was
apparently one of the two young women introduced by Mr Upton
Richards, the newly appointed incumbent of the Margaret Street
Chapel. Referred to in subsequent letters of Mr Dodsworth as Sister
Harriet, she is not to be identified, as was once supposed, with Miss
Harriet Brownlow Byron, likewise a parishioner and later a penitent
of Mr Upton Richards, who with her friend, Miss Ethel Benett, was
at about this time a frequent visitor at No. 17 Park Village West.[1]

Not far from Park Village West, at 154 Albany Street, resided one
of the Wardens of Christ Church, Mr William Madox, the son and
heir of the Mistress of Pitreavie Castle, near Dunfermline, Fife.
The elder of his two daughters, Caroline Augusta, became acquainted
with the Sisters shortly after their establishment in Regent's Park.
Acquaintance with their life of dedication led Miss Madox to desire
to join them in it. In 1852 she dedicated herself to the Religious Life
in the Sisterhood of the Holy Cross but "was obliged by her parents,
to withdraw" from Community life. She continued her connection

[1] The Reverend Mother Superior of the Society of the All Saints Sisters of the Poor,
a Community initiated in 1851 by Miss Byron under the guidance of Mr Upton
Richards, has assured the author that their Foundress was never more than a visitor at
No. 17 Park Village West. The Sister Harriet introduced by Mr Upton Richards in 1846
seems to have been the Sister Harriet mentioned in 1852 by an ex-Sister of the Park
Village Community as being "completely under Mr Richards' influence" and "unfitted in mind and body for such a system" as a Sisterhood. She has been identified
beyond doubt as Harriet Barrand (or Barraud) whose name appears in the Census
return of 1851 as resident in one of the houses in Wyndham Place, Plymouth, occupied by the Sisters of Mercy. The Sister who came to Park Village in 1846 was the
subject of much correspondence between Mr Dodsworth and Mr Richards, and between
Mr Richards and Dr Pusey, in that year and finally, in 1855, between Mr Richards and
Mother Emma, and between Mr Richards and Dr Pusey. Sister Harriet was at various
times between 1847 and 1855 in residence at No. 17 Park Village West, St Saviour's,
Osnaburgh Street, the Home of the All Saints Sisters in Mortimer Street, and Devonport. She is the Sister mentioned in Miss Goodman's *Sisterhoods in the Church of Eng-
land* (p. 41) since the "passage at arms" between Mr Richards and Sister Catherine of
the Devonport Society was the subject of an indignant letter of Mr Richards to Dr
Pusey. Sister Harriet's name is found in the draft list of Sisters of the Devonport
Sisters, prepared by Mother Bertha of that Society, as Harriet Barrand (or Barraud),
"in Religion" Sister Maude, "Sister of the Holy Cross", "not a Sister of the Society of
Devonport—dismissed". "[Admitted by] Dr E. B. Pusey and Rev. Upton Richards".
In a separate column Mother Bertha wrote, "R.I.P." The list was drawn up in 1887.

with the Community, however, as an Associate Sister. On the death of his mother, Mr Madox became Laird of Pitreavie, which necessitated his removal to Scotland and the addition of his mother's family name of Blackwood to his own. On his death in 1863 his elder daughter fell heir to Pitreavie and the care of her step-mother. These responsibilities compelled her to forego the realization of her "desire of becoming a Sister" until such time as she should be free from family obligations. As early as 1856 she was able to associate herself with the Religious Life as an Extern or Third Order Sister of the Society which in that year absorbed the Community with which she was an Associate Sister. The story of her later "steps in Religion" is told in its chronological place in this history.

APPENDED NOTE TO CHAPTER TWO

THE CONTRIBUTION OF
THE SCOTTISH EPISCOPAL CHURCH
TO THE ANGLICAN CONVENTUAL REVIVAL
IN THE NINETEENTH CENTURY

Some credit for the establishment of the Park Village Community must go to the Scottish Episcopal Church, then as now in full communion with the English Church but more explicitly Catholic in its formularies. These formularies made no reference to the Religious Life, but the Episcopalian Sir Walter Scott had helped to prepare the ground with his sympathetic descriptions of medieval monasticism. A more concrete contribution came from St Paul's Church (now Old St Paul's) in the old town of Edinburgh, where the Reverend John Alexander, a converted lawyer, had started work in 1842 on Tractarian lines. This work had the support of the Bishop of Edinburgh, Charles Hughes Terrot, who was also incumbent of St Paul's Church in the New Town. The Bishop and Mr Alexander lived near each other, in Northumberland Street, and there must have been close contact between them. During the winter of 1844 the bishop wrote to Dr Pusey, of the desire of two of his daughters "for greater usefulness, and for more intimate communion with persons whom they could look to as real followers of Christ" than they could find at home—a somewhat grim view for the daughters of a bishop to take of their father's flock. The bishop "despairing of their viewing their present position more favourably gave not a reluctant consent" to their wish to enter a Sisterhood. As related in the text, only one of the Miss Terrots joined the Community when it was actually begun. On the afternoon of Wednesday, 2 April 1845, Sarah Anne Terrot took the London steamer south from Granton Pier outside Edinburgh and arrived at No. 17 Park Village West on the following Friday evening.[1] Miss Terrot was followed in September 1845 by Caroline Augusta Colt, who was a member of Mr Alexander's congregation when her family lived in Edinburgh. (Their estate was at Gartsherrie in Lanarkshire.) Dr Pusey had written on 1 March 1845 that he knew of "seven in Edinburgh alone" who aspired to the Religious Life. While the remaining five cannot be identified with certainty, it is testimony to the reception of Tractarian ideas in the Episcopal Church of Scotland and to the soundness of Mr Alexander's teaching that as many as seven were attracted to the Religious Life as Mr Alexander understood it. This understanding seems to have had its limitation; for Dr Pusey wrote of Mr Alexander on 25 September 1845: "He has, evidently, no idea of conventual life, and so thinks it a mere exchange of one scene of active charity for another." Miss Colt's letters to Dr Pusey, recently discovered, assert that Mr Alexander had no intention of establishing anything like a "convent".

Women of Scottish birth or ancestry who became Sisters of the Holy Cross between 1845 and 1856 were the Hon. Georgiana Napier, who became an Associate Sister in 1847; Miss Katherine Ogilvie, of Boyndlie, Aberdeen; Miss Susanna Logan; Miss Harriet Erskine of Cambo. Miss Mary Bruce and Miss Etheldreda Pillans were of Scottish descent. The second Mother Superior of the Devonport Society of the Most Holy Trinity, Elizabeth Bertha Turnbull, was a Scotswoman, the daughter of a Chamberlain of the City of Edinburgh. Miss Caroline Augusta Madox, a grand-daughter of Mrs Blackwood, mistress of Pitreavie Castle in Fife, was for a time a Probationer or Novice in the Sisterhood of the Holy Cross and eventually became a member of the Devonport Society, first as a Sister of Charity of the Third Order, and finally as a Nun of the Second Order, who dedicated the fortune inherited from her grand-mother after the death of her father, to the completion of the Priory Church at Ascot.

[1] Another daughter of Bishop Terrot, Anna Jemima, became a Sister of Charity of the Devonport Society in the 1860s, and worked for many years in the East End of London. She returned to Scotland towards the end of her life.

3

"What a Sisterhood was Like"
1846

Of the several works contemplated in the confidential prospectus circulated by the Committee of Laymen sponsoring the Sisterhood of Mercy, the two immediately undertaken were "visiting the poor . . . at their own houses", described by Sister Jane Ellacombe in her letter of 1 April 1845, and "feeding, clothing, and instructing destitute children" in the Ragged School conducted by the Sisters "for those children who were too poor or too dirty to be taken into the National School at Christ Church". This Ragged School, wrote Dr Pusey two years later, was

> a great blessing. . . . Unbaptized children, growing up, were prepared for Baptism and gave proofs afterwards in their life of baptismal grace. . . . These children, taken often from bad and careless families, when they were fitted to go to the National School, [were] remarked on by the teachers there as the best children. . . . One effect of the Ragged School was the improvement that became visible in the families where the children attended it. The Sisters gradually won the hearts of the parents through their kindness to the children, and thus the school was a missionary power in the elder generation. . . . Soon even rough, hard-looking men recognized them as "Sisters of Mercy"; and they were called in to cases of sorrow and distress. One person sent them to another.

In a short time, "as it was generally known among the poor that they would gladly go wherever they were wanted", the Sisters gave up routine house-to-house visiting as an unnecessary expenditure of time and strength.

In September 1845, Mr Dodsworth undertook to "see what could be done about the refuge for distressed women" contemplated in the Rule of the Sisterhood. As a preliminary step "he would look into

36

the finances of the Community" and consult with the Committee of Laymen. "He thought also that it would be desirable to have a place for penitents." In November he reported to Dr Pusey that he and Mr Acland, one of the Committee, had "examined into their funds, with the view of engaging a house for the purpose" of sheltering women in distress. Mr Acland thought that "they were not in sufficiently flourishing circumstances" to allow of immediate action.

The Rule of the Sisterhood, as first drafted, gave directions for the reception of women and girls as "Domestic" or Lay Sisters (also called "Serving Sisters"). Frequent mention is made in letters of Mr Dodsworth written between Holy Week 1845 and the end of November 1847, of the proposed or actual admission of one or more aspirants to this rank in the Community. The women and girls so received either were found unsuitable or else withdrew, after a short time, for reasons of health or because of home duties.[1] In the copy of the Manuscript Rule at Ascot, as revised in 1848, there is no provision for Lay Sisters.

The daily life of the Sisters has been described in detail by a Novice who was received into the Community in 1850:

The Sisters rose at five o'clock. . . . The service called Lauds was at six a.m., said in the Oratory . . . at a quarter to seven the Sisters assembled in the same room and Prime was said. . . . Breakfast followed, which was taken in silence; indeed silence was observed all day, except at the hours appointed for recreation. After that meal we said Terce and went to hear Morning Prayers read in the church. . . . The Sisters who taught in the poor school went to their duties. . . . The children were taken to church also. After prayers on their return to the school-room, they were provided with a good meal of rice and milk. In order to insure their exterior attention to the service . . . a rule was made that every child who misbehaved should get no sugar. The rule worked admirably. The school lasted till twelve, when we went home and said Sext. We had dinner at twenty minutes to one, still in silence. The food was plain, good, and sufficient. After dinner we talked together in the Common

---

[1] In 1851 Mr Dodsworth alleged that a "young person who wished to be admitted into the Sisterhood in Regent's Park as a 'Serving Sister' . . . left it because she found . . . that she would be required to use confession". Dr Pusey, in rebuttal of the charge that he made this a condition of admission, mentioned "two persons of that class"— that is, candidates for the rank of Lay Sisters—as having "applied to him for confession". In neither case was subsequent withdrawal due to the supposed requirement. In one case, it was declared to be "weak health and . . . being needed at home". This is the only reference to Lay Sisters in the Park Village Community after 1847.

Room. At three we said None. The Sisters appointed to attend the school ... omitted this service altogether. The school was dismissed for the day at half-past four. At five there were three quarters of an hour for spiritual reading, then Vespers. Supper followed at six o'clock, and after it a few moments' ... recreation. We then prepared for church: ... those who could not go after the fatigues of the day read the service at home. On our return from church at eight o'clock Compline was said, and the Sisters remained in the Oratory after its conclusion for private devotion till twenty minutes past nine, when Mattins was said.[1]

The author of the foregoing account commented that "this order of time worked well and was observed with the utmost regularity".

The habit of the Sisters was described by Dr Pusey, in a letter addressed to Mr Beresford Hope in 1848, as "a very plain, rather coarse, black dress, edged with a little white about the neck". Chapter XVIII of the Rule directs that the Sisters should wear black clothes as simple as possible as to materials and as to form. They should wear neither superfluous trimmings nor anything which does not denote religious simplicity. The material finally adopted was "French merino", supplied to the Park Village Sisters (as also, later, to the Devonport Sisters) by a wool merchant in Leeds associated with St Saviour's Church there. The habit was cut in the shape of a sack. The Sisters "wore under their habit a simple [silver] cross, which opening with a spring disclosed a crucifix". These crosses were obtained from France by Miss Hughes. Dr Pusey wrote to Mr Ellacombe sometime in 1845 that the Sisters had "settled to cut off their hair, as long hair takes so much time", of which they "had none to spare". They wore in the house caps, described by a Novice as "girdled"—whatever that may mean—and also "abroad, as no one saw it", since the Sisters wore bonnets in place of veils. Outside the house the Sisters at first wore cloaks—later shawls. The wearing of a "somewhat distinctive dress", Dr Pusey thought, "was of great

[1] A comparison of the account given above with the timetable of the Sisterhood given by Canon Liddon in the *Life of E. B. Pusey* (Vol. III, p. 24) indicates that between 1845 and 1850 the hour for Matins had been changed from 5.20 a.m. to 9.20 p.m. There were a few other minor changes due to adjustment to changed conditions. It will be noted that the Sisters of the Holy Cross recited a "two-fold" Office: The "daily Service" of Morning and Evening Prayer of the Book of Common Prayer celebrated in Christ Church, and the Day Hours of the Sarum Breviary (in the translation of the Reverend Albany Christie made in 1845), supplemented by an adaptation of the Night Office—Matins—of (apparently) the Roman Breviary, celebrated in the Sisters' Oratory.

value", as it "insured them much respect in the places where they visited". It was no doubt for this reason, among others, that Dr Pusey had opposed any notable alteration in the Sisters' dress when such was urged by Mr Dodsworth in order to allay the "revulsion" caused by Sister Elizabeth Wilcox's indiscretion.

The withdrawal of Miss Wilcox from the Community had contributed in no small degree to the dying down of the "excitement" and "revulsion" which had been aroused against the Sisters. When at the beginning of 1846 she asked to be received back into the Community, it was not only the harm done by her indiscretion in ministering to the poor which led Mr Dodsworth to the decision "that they would act wrongly in receiving her back". Other and far weightier considerations of disposition and of attitude towards authority caused him to think "that in fairness to the great experiment they were making", in which patience and submission to authority were "of all things most essential . . . to success", they ought not to readmit one who "had shown herself wanting" in both those qualities. Dr Pusey had taken a more lenient attitude; but the event proved the rightness of Mr Dodsworth's judgement. Before Dr Pusey's letter, communicating the decision not to readmit her, reached Miss Wilcox, she had been received into the Roman Catholic Church.

The case of Miss Wilcox was the first not only of secession of an Anglican Sister to the Roman Catholic Church, but of many other equally serious difficulties "necessarily involved in the revival of the Religious Life" which were to face Dr Pusey and others concerned with that revival. Dr Pusey "probably hardly realized the gravity and intricacy of those questions", especially such as involved "delicate family relations . . . which he would be called upon to settle, nor the force of prejudice that the Religious Life would not unnaturally excite, nor the difficulty of guiding and restraining the emotional and sensitive characters with whom he would be brought in contact". It must be remembered, as Canon Liddon reminds the readers of his *Life of E. B. Pusey*, "that in England, and in English families, with the exception of the limited circle of the older Roman Catholic families, there had been for centuries literally no experience of the Religious Life. The special vocation of a Sister . . . the character involved and the claims of such a character, were altogether unknown. . . . That young ladies . . . should shrink from 'society', and entertain thoughts of a vow of celibacy in the face of an eligible marriage was almost inconceivable. Besides . . . there was also the notorious jealousy of interference on the part of a spiritual guide in the private arrangements of family life."

The reference to "young ladies who entertained thoughts of a vow of celibacy in the face of an eligible marriage" is based in part on the case of Sister Jane Ellacombe, who (it will be remembered) terminated her engagement of marriage in order to dedicate herself to the virgin state. Miss Ellacombe's father's attitude towards his daughter's embracing the life of a Sister of Mercy was one of reluctance, rather than active opposition, and was overcome before she entered the Sisterhood. The earliest recorded instance of active (and for a time successful) parental opposition occurred in 1846, when the father of Miss Etheldreda Anna Benett, a Wiltshire gentleman of wealth and social prominence, sternly opposed his daughter's association with Dr Pusey. The latter had become acquainted with Miss Benett in 1843, when he and his daughter, Lucy, on holiday at Clifton, occupied lodgings "within two doors" of Miss Benett and her parents. Dr Pusey was already acquainted with Mrs Benett. Although Lucy was only thirteen and Miss Benett nearly six years her senior, their daily walks together, to and from Clifton Church, soon made them close friends. Usually they were accompanied on these walks by Dr Pusey. Lucy was already looking forward to the time when a revival of the Religious Life in the English Church would make possible the realization of her desire to be a "Sister of Mercy". Her communication of this desire to her friend seems to have inspired the latter to look forward to a like dedication. One can have no doubt that Dr Pusey would do all in his power to foster Miss Benett's aspiration.

Letters of spiritual counsel continued Dr Pusey's contact with his young friend after he and Lucy returned to Oxford and Miss Benett to Pyt House, near Tisbury, in Wiltshire. When Mr Benett learned of this correspondence, he forbade further communication between his daughter and Dr Pusey. He was particularly opposed to her resorting to Dr Pusey for sacramental confession. A long letter from Dr Pusey to Mr Benett has been preserved, written in 1846, in which he strove to allay the anxious father's fears of undue influence over his daughter rising from an imagined romantic attachment between Miss Benett and her spiritual guide: arguing for her right, since she was now of age, to avail herself of the liberty insured by the first

Exhortation in the Prayer Book Communion Office to resort to a "discreet and learned Minister of God's Word . . . [for] the benefit of Absolution".

In deference to Mr Benett's persistent objection, the correspondence seems to have come to an end. But Miss Benett, during her father's residence in London as M.P., availed herself of her liberty and right to make her confession to Dr Pusey at Christ Church, with the approval of Mr Dodsworth. By the end of 1846 or the early part of 1847 her father's opposition was so far abated that Miss Benett was able to make an extended visit at No. 17 Park Village West, during which she is said to have been "among the Sisters" in a context which implies that she was "among them" as a member of the Community. Dr Pusey, as early as January 1846, had referred to Miss Benett as "Ethel . . . our future 'Sister', if God will". It is now impossible to say whether Miss Benett was actually "received as a Sister" (however informally) during her visit in Park Village West at this time. The Superior of the Society of the Sisters of Bethany, in reply to an inquiry addressed to her in 1945, was emphatic in her assertion that their Foundress had never been a Sister of the Holy Cross or any other Community prior to her novitiate in the All Saints Community in preparation for the founding of the Sisterhood in Lloyd Square. Her early association with Dr Pusey and Park Village West was acknowledged. Sister Clara, who was a frequent visitor at No. 17 Park Village West before her actual reception as a Sister in the autumn of 1847, states definitely in her reminiscences of the early years of the Sisterhood that "she who was later Foundress of the Sisters of Bethany was among the Sisters" in the Park Village Community.[1]

Whatever was the nature of Miss Benett's association with the Community, it came to an end within the year 1847, no doubt in consequence of her father's renewed or intensified opposition. It was not until his death in 1864 that Miss Benett was free to embrace the life to which she had been inspired by Lucy Pusey to dedicate

[1] Sister Clara's statement is as follows: "Several now [1889 or 1890] in high responsible offices in other Communities began their first attempt at Park Village. . . . She who was later Foundress of the Sisters of Bethany was among the Sisters." Dr Pusey's reference to "Ethel" as "our future 'Sister', if God will" is too indefinite to be cited in support of a claim that Mother Ethel was actually a member of the Community. Her possession of a copy of the original Rule indicates an intimate relation to the Sisterhood.

herself twenty-one years before. After a Novitiate made in the Community of her friend, Mother Harriet Brownlow Byron of the Society of the All Saints Sisters of the Poor, Margaret Street, Miss Benett founded in 1866, in Lloyd Square, Pentonville, London, the Society in the Sisters of Bethany.

4

Growth and Expansion
1847—1848

In the Spring of 1847 the Committee of Laymen was faced with the imminent necessity of providing additional accommodation for the growing Community and its projected works. No steps had been taken towards the reception of distressed women or the care of orphans or penitents. The invalidism of Sister Jane, Sister Mary, and Sister Caroline made it imperative to provide an infirmary for their care. The house in Park Village West—already "too small for invalids", as Mr Dodsworth observed in a letter to Dr Pusey written in Ascensiontide 1847—would soon be taxed beyond its capacity by the arrival, "almost immediately expected", of three young women in whom Dr Pusey had fostered a desire for the Religious Life. Lord Clive and Mr Gladstone were delegated by the Committee of Laymen to consider the desirability of taking on lease a "second house" to accommodate the invalids. The premises inspected by them in company with Mr Dodsworth were deemed less suitable than No. 17. "Gladstone strongly inclined to the purchase of [the latter], if they could obtain permission from [the Commissioners of] 'Woods and Forests', and to build another house adjoining." Mr Dodsworth was "disposed to think that this would be the best thing to do". The permission of the Commissioners was apparently withheld. For the present the plan of purchasing property in the Regent's Park district was abandoned. Accommodation was provided for Dr Pusey's three "new Sisters" by the departure of two of the invalids.

Sister Caroline left the Community to be received on 2 July into the Roman Catholic Church.[1] Sister Mary Bruce's health had been

---

[1] Miss Colt's ill health seems to have been due mainly to emotional and credal tensions. After her reception into the Roman Catholic Church her health was sufficiently restored for her to pass through the rigours of a Carmelite novitiate to Life Profession in

"very bad" as early as the summer of 1845, when Dr Pusey "spent much time ministering to her in his vacation". In the summer of 1847 she was obliged to leave the Community altogether. She went for change of air to Hayling Island off the Hampshire coast, where Dr Pusey and his two surviving children, Mary and Philip, were spending their holiday. Another visitor at Hayling was Miss Marian Hughes. Miss Hughes was still unable to be received formally into the Sisterhood which owed much to the counsel and practical assistance which she rendered to Dr Pusey in drafting its Rule and fashioning its observances.[1] A compromise, however, was arranged with Dr Pusey's co-operation, by which Miss Hughes "would spend part of Lent and Easter [of 1848] at the Sisterhood in Park Village". She was to be "admitted as a Sister . . . to live under their Rule, while she was able to be away from her mother". She left Hayling in September 1847 with the Puseys, stopping in London to pay a visit to the Sisterhood in Regent's Park and "to be introduced to the Mother and Sisters".

During the summers of 1847 and 1848, when Dr Pusey and his children were at Hayling, there were frequent interchanges of visits between the members of the household on the island and the family of Dr Pusey's friend, the Reverend Edward T. Richards, vicar of the neighbouring parish of Farlington on the mainland. Mr Richards' eldest daughter, Charlotte, through association at this time with Dr Pusey, Sister Mary Bruce, and Miss Hughes, was encouraged to look forward to the time when she could realize the desire already inspired by her cousin, Helen Richards, one of the young people on holiday on the Hampshire coast, to embrace the Religious Life. Helen Richards had been at school with Lucy Pusey at Clifton. The two were "almost the first of the band of young girls who thought of dedicating themselves as Sisters of Mercy"—an aspiration which was realized in 1850 when Charlotte Richards was received as a Novice of the Devonport Society.

1851 in the Carmel at Warrenmount, Dublin, where in 1907, at the age of eighty-seven, she died, as she had lived, in the odour of Carmelite sanctity. Her Sisters in Carmel record that she often told them of the austere life lived by "the Anglican Nuns and of the penances they performed".

[1] It was Miss Hughes who "got the Sisters some crosses like those she had seen" in France, which "they all wore"—small silver crosses "which opened and had [inside] a figure of Christ crucified" (as described by Miss Goodman in *Sisterhoods in the Church of England*, p. 206, cf. p. 38 above). It was she whom Dr Pusey consulted as to details of dress.

Sister Mary Bruce remained a member of Dr Pusey's household at Christ Church as a chaperone-governess to Mary Pusey until Miss Pusey's marriage in July 1854 to the Reverend James G. Brine. Miss Hughes, who was often at Christ Church at this time, thought that a secular governess "would have been better for her. To Philip", however, Dr Pusey's afflicted son, Sister Mary "was a great comfort and true friend". After a winter spent in Scotland with the Dowager Duchess of Argyll at Ardencaple Castle, Sister Mary's health was so far "recruited" that in 1855 she was able to undertake work in Dundee under Bishop Forbes as "Superior" of an institution for the training of school-mistresses. There Dr John Mason Neale met her in the autumn of 1855. For a time she helped Provost Fortescue at St Ninian's Cathedral in Perth. In her later years she lived in London, supported by Dr Pusey and Mother Ethel Benett of the Society of the Sisters of Bethany, whom she had known when the latter was "among the Sisters" in Park Village West, and by legacies of Bishop Forbes and the former Provost Fortescue. She died on 30 April 1878, at the age of sixty-six, in the University College Hospital, London. There she was nursed by the All Saints Sisters of the Poor, whose Foundress, Mother Harriet Brownlow Byron, had known Sister Mary since early days in Regent's Park. Sister Mary was attended in her last hours by another friend of Park Village days, Sister Georgina Mary Hoare of the Community of St John Baptist. Father Benson, s.s.j.e., reporting that her funeral had been held in the chapel of the All Saints Sisters in Margaret Street, noted that until the end of her life Sister Mary kept a rule of "something like twelve hours' devotion daily". For all her capacity for devotion, Dr Pusey seemed to consider Sister Mary unsuited for Community life. "She was but a short time a Sister", he wrote in November 1854. "She gets on very well with people when she takes a liking to them. With others she does not get on. And she takes strong prejudices. She would manage *things* very well. I doubt her managing *minds* very well until she herself knows what it is to be under rule." He advised that before undertaking the management of others—perhaps the institute for school-mistresses—"it would be best for her to be under authority, as at Clewer".

The departure of Sister Caroline and Sister Mary reduced the number of Sisters from the seven mentioned by Mr Dodsworth in his letter of 3 December 1845 to four or five: Mother Emma, Sister

Jane, Sister Sarah Anne, Sister Etheldreda, and Mr Upton Richards' spiritual child, Sister Harriet. Dr Pusey's three aspirants were expected as early as Ascensiontide. For one reason or another their coming had been delayed. Two of the aspirants were from Scotland— the Hon. Georgiana Louisa Napier of Merchiston Castle, near Edinburgh, one of the "seven from Edinburgh" mentioned by Dr Pusey, and Miss Katherine Ogilvie of Boyndlie-by-Fraserburg, Aberdeenshire. Miss Ogilvie's coming was delayed until she could fulfil an obligation previously incurred. When that obstacle was cleared, Mrs Ogilvie herself "brought her daughter . . . up to London, to present her", she wrote, "not to the Queen but to the Lord".

The third young lady expected was Miss Helen Ind, the daughter of a wealthy brewer of Romford, Essex. She was a friend of Miss Clarissa Powell, another aspirant, with whom she had been in correspondence as early as 1844 on the subject of her desire to be a Sister of Mercy. She came to the Sisterhood, probably at the time when she was expected. But after some three years of residence in Park Village West, Dr Pusey sent her to Oxford to live with Miss Hughes in her newly established Society of the Holy and Undivided Trinity. Miss Ind's father was opposed to his daughter's becoming a Sister. Under strong paternal pressure she left Miss Hughes in October 1850. Many years afterwards Miss Powell, writing to a friend, made inquiry about "our former Sister, Helen Ind". In the 1860s the name of Miss H. Ind appears in a list of ladies who undertook to help in sundry ways the Devonport Sisters, Miss Ind by finding purchasers for the paintings of Sister Clara, the former Miss Powell.

The Hon. Georgiana Louisa Napier was the second daughter of the eighth Baron Napier, a direct descendant of John Napier of Merchistoun, the inventor of logarithms, and a sister of Lord Francis Patrick Napier, ninth Baron of Napier and Ettrick, Envoy Extraordinary and Minister Plenipotentiary to Washington from 1857 to 1858. Miss Napier, like Sister Jane, Sister Etheldreda, and Miss Powell was a gifted linguist, corresponding with her brother by postcards written in elegant Latin. Like her brother, she was a charming person, spreading love and happiness wherever she might be, of medium height, fair haired and of fair complexion, with beautiful blue eyes that sparkled with humour, and cheeks "of the colour of

No. 46 Albany Street

St Saviour's Home
Osnaburgh Street

Miss Clarissa Powell, *c.* 1844

ripe peaches".[1] She was in her twenty-ninth year when she came to the Sisterhood. The marriages of two of her sisters in the following summer made it necessary for Sister Georgiana, as she was known in Religion, to sacrifice for the present her heart's desire and to return to Scotland to care for her widowed mother. Like Mother Marian Hughes in similar circumstances she was admitted to the Community as an "Associate Sister", following a Rule adapted to the conditions under which such a Sister must live.[2] She was always reckoned to have been "in Religion" during the nine years which passed between her brief sojourn at No. 17 Park Village West in 1847 and her reception as a Sister of Charity of the Devonport Society in 1856. In 1864 she was able to make her Profession as a Sister of Mercy of the same Society. But it was not until after the death of her mother in 1883 that she could be received as a Nun of the Company of the Love of Jesus—thirty-six years after her brief residence in Park Village West. Between 1847 and 1856, whenever she was in London she spent as much time as possible "among the Sisters" as a visitor.[3]

Miss Ogilvie, to be known in Religion as Sister Katherine, was twenty-seven years old, the elder daughter of Dr John Ogilvie of Aberdeen and of Jane Forbes, heiress of Boyndlie, a distant relative of the Reverend Alexander Penrose Forbes, Dr Pusey's friend, who was consecrated bishop of the Scottish Diocese of Brechin a few months after his cousin was "received as a Sister". Sister Katherine's history after her reception into the Sisterhood in 1847, long shrouded in anonymity or concealed behind the veil of the initial "O" of her family name, has only recently been pieced together. It is recorded in the chronological order of its incidents in this history of the Regent's Park Sisterhood.

The last of the aspirants received into the Sisterhood in 1847 was Miss Clarissa Powell, of Foxlease Park, New Forest, and Wilverly Hall near Lymington, Hants, the elder daughter of the late Captain Henry Weyland Powell of the First Grenadiers, a veteran of Quatre-

---

[1] This description of Miss Napier's personal appearance was given to the author by one of the Sisters at Ascot Priory (now gone to her rest) who knew her well.

[2] A summary of this Rule is given at the end of Appendix 2, p. 146.

[3] Miss Napier is so designated in the return for No. 17 Park Village West in the Census of 1851. In 1861 her name appears in the census return for St Saviour's, Osnaburgh Street, with the designation, "A Sister of Charity". Between this date and 1864 she was a Child of the Second Order.

E

Bras. Miss Powell had been for several years—since 1843—under the spiritual direction of Dr Pusey. His enthusiasm for the revival of the Religious Life had awakened in her a desire to dedicate herself to God in Holy Religion. Her mother's opposition, however, made it impossible for her to join the other young women whom Dr Pusey had been training when they inaugurated the Sisterhood of the Holy Cross in the Easter Week of 1845. The time of waiting for her mother's consent was not wasted. During the years 1844, 1845, and 1846 she was engaged in translating for Dr Pusey's "Library of Devotion for English Churchmen" Avrillon's *Guides* to Advent and Lent (1844) and Surin's *Foundations of the Spiritual Life* (1844).[1] For among the "varied accomplishments" with which Miss Powell was endowed a knowledge of foreign languages is mentioned by one of her contemporaries, along with her talent for music, painting, and embroidery. She has been described as being of a "cheerful, amiable disposition", small of stature, "a brunette with large lustrous eyes", and at the age of twenty-eight "very pretty". Underlying these obvious endowments was a deep spirituality, a capacity for ascetic practice and mystical experience, which long years of Dr Pusey's teaching and direction were to bring to fair flowering and rich fruitage.[2]

During the Lent of 1847, at Dr Pusey's suggestion Miss Powell went to Park Village West for a visit. During her stay she enjoyed the privilege of a "retreat",[3] for which she was "very grateful". In the following July her mother's consent was given, and preparations were made, for her admission as a Sister in the autumn. The Reception

[1] It is known positively that Avrillon's *Guides* were translated by Miss Powell, to whom the editor (Dr Pusey) refers in the original form of the Preface to the *Guide to Passing Lent Holily* as "the unknown translator" for whom are asked the prayers of those who may have "found profit to their souls from this little book", "that she may have part with them in the blessedness of knowing and loving God". There is evidence, also, that Surin's work was translated by Miss Powell. Others of the series were translated by Sister Jane Ellacombe and Sister Etheldreda Pillans, Avrillon's *Year of Affections* by Miss Marian Hughes.

[2] Many—perhaps most—of the conversations and letters of which "fragments" form Part IV of *The Spiritual Letters of Edward Bouverie Pusey* (p. 295–344) were either written or spoken to Miss Powell. Transcripts of Dr Pusey's letters to Miss Powell, written between 1844 and 1882, fill three volumes of Dr Pusey's letters preserved at Pusey House. Many of these appear whole or in part in *The Spiritual Letters*.

[3] An idea of the character of this "retreat" may be gained from the account given below (p. 70) by Miss Cusack of what she was told was a "retreat" in preparation for her reception as a "Probationer" in 1850.

took place on the Feast of St Michael and All Angels accompanied by the taking or renewal of the Three Vows of Religion. For which reason the Feast of Michaelmas 1847 was reckoned as the date of Sister Clara's Profession.

Shortly after her reception into the Community, Sister Clara wrote to her mother a detailed account of the life and work at No. 17 Park Village West, especially their ministry to the poor of the district.

> Here we have much to do for our poor, for our hours of visiting are quite filled with going to *very* poor people who want instruction and comforting as well as food and clothes. We are able to give the first from the church, but in very little quantities and what can be spared from the house by way of messes[1] and broth. Then we have the little school [where] the children are fed. . . . It is very pleasant to see the poor little things, they enjoy it so much. The other day we had a very pleasant surprise, a large packet with near a dozen flannel petticoats, shirts, gowns, frocks and baby-clothes. They will not go far with so many; but it was a very pleasant beginning of things sent in for the winter.

It was at this time that another aspirant was received into the Sisterhood: Miss Charlotte Cordelia White, a parishioner of Mr Dodsworth, one of the spiritual children of his mentioned by Sister Clara in her reminiscences as having been introduced by him subsequently to 1845. Miss White was a daughter of the late Sir John Chambers White, Vice-Admiral R.N., whose fortune, consisting for the most part of \$1,000,000 (Spanish) taken as booty from an enemy ship in Spanish waters, he bequeathed (at least in part) to his daughter at his death in 1845. It was to Sister Charlotte that Mother Emma gave, at the time of her reception into the Sisterhood, *Les Entrétiens* of St Francis de Sales, to the grave concern of Mr Dodsworth.[2]

---

[1] The sound and implication of this word are worse than the reality. Scraps of food left over from a meal—"left-overs"—were converted into "made-over" dishes which were far from unsavoury and were certainly nourishing. The broth was *not* made after Mrs Beaton's recipe for "charity-soup".

[2] Many of Mr Dodsworth's letters to Dr Pusey express the concern and disapproval with which he regarded the latter's introduction into the Sisterhood of "unadapted" Roman Catholic treatises on the Religious Life. This was one of the several practices of his former colleague which Mr Dodsworth roundly condemned in his "open letter" to Dr Pusey published after Mr Dodsworth's reception into the Church of Rome in 1851. The Reverend A. M. Allchin in his valuable work, *The Silent Rebellion* (p. 64) attributes Mr Dodsworth's disagreement with Dr Pusey in this matter to "their

At the close of 1847 there were eight Sisters in residence at No. 17 Park Village West: Mother Emma, Sister Jane (still known as Sister Anne), and Sisters Sarah Anne Terrot, Etheldreda Pillans, Katherine Ogilvie, Charlotte White, Clara Powell, and Mr Upton Richards' spiritual child, Sister Harriet Barraud. Miss Napier, as an Associate Sister, was still reckoned a member of the Sisterhood, although not resident. Miss Marian Hughes was in the same case, and perhaps (for the present) Sister Mary Bruce. It was in this year, 1847, that Miss Mary Kebbel, the sister of a some-time Governor of the Castle at Oxford, became acquainted with the Sisterhood of the Holy Cross, when she went to Park Village West for an interview with Dr Pusey. It was not until 1852 or some time later that she was received as a Probationer. An account of her brief novitiate is given in its chronological place in this history.

The problem of housing future accessions to the Sisterhood continued to press on the Committee of Laymen for early action. Sometime before 9 December 1847, an offer was made to the Committee through its secretary, Mr Alexander Beresford-Hope, who was also a Trustee of Margaret Street Chapel, to grant to the Sisterhood of the Holy Cross, rent free, the occupancy of one of the houses adjacent to the "old Chapel", on whose site it was proposed to build the present All Saints' Church. This offer was made on condition that, when the building of the new church was commenced, the Committee "use its best endeavours to purchase the fee simple of sufficient site adjacent to it for the erection of a . . . permanent residence of the Sisters . . . according to the designs of the architect of the new church[1] . . . all legal expenses of such purchase being promised by the same individual who had undertaken [the expenses of] the new church"— to wit, Mr Beresford-Hope himself. Mr Dodsworth was to "retain the superintendence of the establishment as before".[2] A resolution

---

fundamentally different attitudes toward the Church of England. For Dodsworth loyalty to the Church of England involved agreement with her as she then was, while for Pusey loyalty did not seem incompatible with a desire to introduce very deep alterations into her." Dr Pusey "was acting on the principles of the English Church when claiming, as the best Anglican writers had claimed, that the spiritual endowments of the whole Catholic Body belonged to the English portion of it no less than to the rest" (Liddon, *Life of E. B. Pusey*, Vol. III, p. 26).

[1] William Butterfield.

[2] The Committee of Laymen seem, at this early date at least, not to have known of the internal ordering of the Sisterhood by which Mr Dodsworth's "superintendence"

was drafted accepting the "said offer" and sent to Mr Dodsworth for approval. The latter was "inclined to think that it would be better to make the Institution [in Margaret Street] additional to [the house already occupied by] the Sisterhood, rather than as a substitute for it. . . . In any case he could not undertake the superintendence at such a distance. And if he could, he would scarcely feel it right to Richards to do so, although he would give any assistance in his power when his counsel was called for".[1]

In an interview with Mr Upton Richards, which the latter thought "rather unsatisfactory", Mr Dodsworth proposed that the "*sick* Sisters who could do nothing" be sent to Margaret Street, "whilst he kept the able-bodied in Christ Church district". To this Mr Richards declared "he would never consent". Mr Dodsworth urged that the Committee, before adopting Mr Beresford-Hope's proposal, "ascertain . . . the full extent to which the resolution would pledge their funds". The resolution was not adopted and the Margaret Street negotiations came to an end, as also, apparently, did Mr Richards' association with the Park Village Sisterhood as a "coadjutor" to Dr Pusey.

It is impossible to ascertain, from the sources of information now available, whether the Margaret Street project was abandoned before or after the early months of 1848. The last letter extant dealing with

---

was confined to the ordering of the external activities of the Sisters, while Dr Pusey was the "spiritual superintendent". A memorandum preserved at Ascot Priory names Dr Pusey as "Founder" and the Reverend Messrs. Dodsworth and Upton Richards as "Coadjutors". (See the letter of Sister Jane Ellacombe, quoted on p. 23 above, written shortly after the inauguration of the Sisterhood in 1845, in which she stated that Mr Dodsworth "ordered all about their visiting", and the letter from Dr Pusey to Miss Marian Hughes, quoted by Miss Trench in *The Story of Dr Pusey's Life*, p. 270, in which he wrote: "The Sisters are only in their external works under Mr D., who tells them whom they are to visit.") Sister Clara, in her Reminiscences, noted that excepting the Sisters "introduced" by Mr Dodsworth, Mr Upton Richards, and "another priest" (not named), "all had the privilege of having Dr Pusey for their father. He was considered as the Founder and his office was that of Spiritual Superintendent." The arrangement was made at Mr Dodsworth's own request, as has been noted on p. 30 above (note).

[1] As early as September 1845 Dr Pusey wrote to Miss Hughes (in a letter already quoted in part in Chapter 2, p. 30 above, that "the house [in Park Village West], which was a small one, holding only ten, would probably soon overflow, and then, by God's blessing, another Sisterhood was to be formed near Margaret Chapel, but in harmony with [the already existing Community]", adding that "this was, however, not spoken of yet".

the subject bears no other date than the day of the week. Other and more serious problems, however, faced Dr Pusey, Mr Dodsworth, and the members of the Committee of Laymen. Bishop Blomfield had never committed himself to positive approval of the Sisterhood. In a letter dated 28 April 1845, about a month after the Sisters went into residence, Mr Dodsworth reported to Dr Pusey that he had "a short talk with the Bishop of London about the [Sisterhood]". The Bishop was "very anxious that they should have a limit as to age: he objected to any young persons entering: perhaps under thirty". Mr Dodsworth thought that he "seemed as favourably disposed as he could have expected". "We must try", Mr Dodsworth added, "to strike out of the Rules what would offend him, so that no essential point is sacrificed." The Rule was accordingly revised with a view to submission to the Bishop whenever he should ask to see it.

The Rule as originally drafted is represented by extracts from a copy in the possession of Mother Ethel Benett which she sent to Canon Liddon for inspection at the time of his writing the life of Dr Pusey. These extracts, transcribed as marginal notes in a copy of the Rule preserved at Pusey House in a volume of correspondence between Dr Pusey and Mr A. J. Beresford-Hope, embody the passages "stricken out of the Rules" by Dr Pusey and Mr Dodsworth in 1845 as likely to offend the Bishop.[1] In the letter to Mr Beresford-Hope dated Quinquagesima 1848, of which we have already quoted a part,[2] Dr Pusey gave the following account of the principle and procedure followed in drafting the Rule in its original form, its alteration by Dr Pusey and Mr Dodsworth, and its submission to Mr Keble for comment and suggestion:

> We naturally went by experience. Lord John Manners procured us the Rules of the Sisters of [Mercy] at Birmingham. I had some rules by me, used by different bodies in England and on the continent. We took as our basis St Augustine's Rule, as extant in an Epistle of his to some "Sanctimoniales" whom he had brought together; thinking it most in

[1] The passages "stricken out" are principally such as state or imply that the Sisters are "Spouses of Christ" or that our Lord is their Spouse (one such passage being an ejaculation on receiving Holy Communion based on the opening words of the Song of Songs), the explicit mention, with specific directions, of the "use of Confession", and one long section of the chapter "Of Holy Communion" in which the union of the soul of the communicant with our Lord is likened to the union of the Blessed Virgin with our Lord after his conception, and the communicant is encouraged to use ejaculations suggestive of the ardent language of the Song of Songs. (See Appendix 2, p. 137.)

[2] See p. 15 above.

accordance with our Church to take rules from one of the Fathers of the Church. On this we engrafted others, always bearing in mind the character of English Churchwomen. When it was done, Dodsworth and myself looked over it, with a view to what the Bishop of London would think; and several little points were altered (language, chiefly) on his saying, "The Bishop would not like that". This was kept to be shown to the Bishop, whenever trial enough had been made of the institution for him to be ready to take it up. *We could not bring it before him sooner, without asking him to do the very thing* which he naturally did not wish to do yet. For if he saw the rules and sanctioned them, the Sisterhood would have been at once under his sanction. This we wished but could not ask for. When we had thus reviewed the rules, we showed them to John Keble.

The other rules "engrafted" on the Rule of St Augustine were sections of the *Spiritual Directory*, and many passages from the *Constitutions*, of the Nuns of the Visitation, and certain features adapted from the regulations of the Roman Catholic Sisters of Mercy.[1] As revised by Dr Pusey and Mr Dodsworth and observed by the Sisters until further revision in 1848, "the Rule of the Sisterhood [of the Holy Cross] consisted . . . of thirty-three chapters, which are not so much a dry code of regulations as a series of spiritual exhortations". In a letter to Dr John Mason Neale, written in 1855, the Reverend W. J. Butler, founder of the Community of St Mary the Virgin, Wantage, described the Regent's Park Rules as "short sermons, expansions of St Augustine's Rule", adding that "the advantage of a sermonic Rule is that the reading of it gives a devotional atmosphere to the house".

The cautiously noncommittal attitude of Bishop Blomfield towards the Sisterhood, noted by Mr Dodsworth in reporting his interview with the Bishop in April 1845, was by the end of 1847 taking the form of what he was to declare in 1850 to be definite "objections to the Sisterhood" as at that time conducted. His Lordship's "objections" were based specifically on the use by the Sisters of "the books

---

[1] On 15 April, 1845, Mr Dodsworth wrote to Dr Pusey: "So far as I have examined the books, it seems to me that we may take the Birmingham Rules"—that is, the Rule of the Roman Catholic Sisters of Mercy—"as the foundation, and they really require very little alteration. Only we must add to them 'Distribution of Time' and from our MS. 'Care of the Body' and 'Diet'. . . . Also I wish to suggest whether we might omit that part 'On Holy Communion' which draws a parallel between our Lord's conception and of the Holy Ghost being conceived within us. I know this would offend the Bishop." This passage was not omitted, however, until the revision of 1848. It is in Mother Ethel's MS. copy and Sister Clara's version.

of devotion which Dr Pusey had adapted from writers of the Church of Rome", and also the fact that the Sisterhood "should be almost wholly under the guidance of a clergyman not in any way connected with his diocese".[1] Further grounds upon which he "felt it to be his duty to withhold his approval from the Sisterhood" was that "its tone and tendency appeared to him to be towards Rome". It was "during this crisis that Mr Beresford-Hope was employed by Dr Pusey as an intermediary" and in the Spring of 1848 made what Mr Beresford-Hope reported as "peace", but which in the event proved to be on the Bishop's part a grudging truce. "Toward this [end] Mr Beresford-Hope claimed to see and show (as he did) a copy of the Rule to the Bishop. . . . The Bishop read the Rule and returned it . . . without comment." The copy of the Rule shown to the Bishop is the one now at Pusey House among the Pusey–Hope papers.

Besides the Rule, the Offices used by the Sisters in their corporate devotions would eventually have to be submitted to the Bishop for approval, as the understanding with the lay promoters of the Sisterhood was "that the whole institution would be open to the Bishop". In the light of the Bishop's avowed disapproval of the private devotions provided for the Sisters in Dr Pusey's "adapted books", Mr Dodsworth and Mr Beresford-Hope had reason to apprehend that the Bishop would not approve of the forms of corporate prayer provided for them. Of the "adapted" books of private devotion, Dr Pusey wrote to Mr Beresford-Hope in 1848, that "he admitted whatever he believed to be true, believing it also not contrary to the teaching of the Church of England". As for the adaptation of the Offices of the Breviary for the corporate prayer of the Sisterhood, "he knew of no resource in providing for frequent offices but to go to the source from which our English Prayer Book is taken, and to give them such devotions as he felt sure they could use in the Bishop's presence. . . . There was nothing that was not framed on the service of the Church of England." In the Lessons to be read at Mattins "there was no passage from any Father which he could not himself preach in a sermon before the Bishop, nor any prayer which the Bishop himself might not use". All legendary matter was omitted from the Nocturn Lessons, invocation of Saints was excluded; not even the prayer for the faithful departed at the end of the Offices was

[1] Dr Pusey was canonically attached to the Diocese of Oxford.

retained, although in the course of time the practice arose of the Sisters making a pause and saying the prayer mentally.

Dr Pusey and the Sisters, no less than Mr Dodsworth and the members of the Committee of Laymen, would have "esteemed it a great gain to have the Bishop's blessing, and feel that they and their labours were owned and sanctioned by the Church through him". The most that was gained, however, from the intermediation of Mr Beresford-Hope seems to have been that the Bishop, after having returned the copy of the Rule "without comment", on further consideration relented so far as to tell Mr Beresford-Hope "that he saw nothing to object to, if wisely and judiciously carried out, and that he would say so to any who complained to him. This", Dr Pusey thought, "was a great gain."

Meantime the number of the Sisters had so far increased that by the summer of 1848 the problems of accommodating the increasing numbers and of beginning the long-delayed expansion of their work resumed the primary importance which for a time had been eclipsed by anxiety about episcopal approval. The first step towards solving the two closely allied problems was made possible by the offer of Sister Charlotte White of £100 annually towards the rent of an additional house and other expenses and a further annual grant of £100 towards the maintenance of orphans, whose reception and training had been one of the activities envisaged by the Committee of Laymen. Sister Charlotte undertook to "gather" the orphans and to devote herself to their care. It was in August 1848 that "a house in Albany Street" "was taken and fitted up for [the orphans] and other purposes". The house was No. 46 Upper Albany Street, "a few doors north of the church" and at a greater distance south of Park Village West.[1] Here

[1] Miss Cusack, who was resident in the Sisterhood between 1850 and 1854, and the Reverend H. W. Burrows, who succeeded Mr Dodsworth in the incumbency of Christ Church in 1851, state that the Sisters occupied *two* houses—Miss Cusack adds, "in the same street". A later incumbent refers to one of the houses occupied by the Sisters as having been at a subsequent date the home of Christina Rossetti and her mother and sister. This was No. 45, adjoining No. 46, taken by William Rossetti in 1854 for his mother and sisters. There is no substantiation in Census returns or other relevant documents that the Sisters ever occupied No. 45. Miss Cusack's statement that the two houses occupied by the Sisters were "in the same street"—she does not say that they were adjoining—may be due to the fact that she considered Park Village West to be a "serpentine" extension of Upper Albany Street. In a manuscript memorandum at Ascot Priory in which many minor errors have been detected, due to lapses of memory on the part of the narrator, certain Sisters bearing the names of Sisters known to have

were housed four orphan girls, "gathered" by Sister Charlotte, to-
gether with Sister Etheldreda who held the office of "Mistress of the
Orphans", Sister Charlotte herself, and Sister Clara. Reference is
made to Sister Clara's residence at No. 46 in a letter of Mr Dodsworth,
dated 24 October, in which he complained of finding a copy of one of
St Alphonsus Liguori's books—no doubt *The True Spouse of Jesus
Christ*—on a table in the Common Room of No. 46, which work
Mother Emma assured Mr Dodsworth was for Sister Clara's use only.

It was at this time that the first "distressed woman" to be received
was "accidentally found and rescued from suicide to which she was
being driven by poverty". She was given shelter in Park Village West.
On St Matthew's Day (21 September) 1848 Sister Jane Ellacombe
(now no longer called Sister Anne) wrote to her sister from No. 17
Park Village West: "We now have a second large house ... between
this and the church"; adding, "One hopes, please God, to have a
large house built so that we can all be together again". In the same
letter Sister Jane bade her sister, "Pray ... for one of us who is now
very seriously ill at the other house. The Superior and one other
Sister are constantly with her." The sick Sister was Sister Etheldreda,
who "in the summer of 1848 contracted small-pox", which was at
first thought to be scarlet fever. Although described by one of the
Sisters as being "of the worst kind", it was "mitigated by vaccination".
As Dr Pusey had himself been vaccinated "though inoculation",
and so "was not liable to it, and ... would not carry it", he proposed
to go to London the next day (September 19) to administer Holy
Communion to the sick Sister. In the meantime Mr Upton Richards
was ministering to her. One morning he found "that Sister Etheldreda had been wandering in mind in the night and was ... asserting
that she was not Sister Etheldreda. . . . The Mother doubted whether
it would be advisable to celebrate. Mr Richards suggested, however,
that he might at least celebrate and the rest receive if she seemed con-

---

been members of the Park Village Community are referred to as the "Onslow Square
Sisters". As Onslow Square is in Brompton, some three miles from Regent's Park, and
no traces can be found in contemporary census returns of Sisters living in that district
at the time, one is tempted to surmise that "Onslow Square" is a *lusus memoriae* for a
location which cannot at present be identified. It is significant, however, that in the
Census of 1851 several of the Sisters named as "Onslow Square Sisters", known to have
been members of the Regent's Park Community, are not listed among the Sisters resident at No. 17 Park Village West or elsewhere in the Regent's Park district.

scious. And so they did celebrate and she did receive it so reverently that it quite affected them all. Mr Richards felt that though she did not know herself, she would know her Lord; and so it was. . . . At the close, before leaving the room, he commended her specially to God, her lips moved and she responded 'Amen' ". When Dr Pusey arrived on 20 September, he set about at once to assist Mother Emma and the Sister in nursing Sister Etheldreda. "For hours he went about searching for a person who would shave her head, and he assisted at that painful sight himself, as if she were his own child. He celebrated daily in the Infirmary near the sick bed." In spite of vaccination "the disease was very severe and it was judged that her strength would not hold out till the time at which the fever would turn. She was lying apparently unconscious. . . . Still [Dr Pusey] thought it possible that she might receive the Blessed Sacrament; at least he would try. He approached the bed and—she suddenly raised herself, as if awakening, and received the Precious Body and Blood, and from that moment began to recover." Although her health was never fully restored, she was able to continue her duties as Mistress of the Orphans, to which post she had been appointed shortly before her illness.

Although Sister Etheldreda held the office of "Mistress of the Orphans" and Sister Charlotte had immediate oversight of them, it was Mother Emma who "organized their rule after the model of Port Royal".[1] As Superior she retained frequent contact with them, for she wrote to Dr Pusey in 1848: "It is incredible what power we have over young women and children when we have them in the house"—in implied contrast with the difficulty of controlling the urchins of the Ragged School and their sisters. The younger children

[1] The authority for this statement as to the rule of the Regent's Park Orphanage is the memorandum already cited, found in the archives at Ascot Priory, entitled "The Order of the Holy Cross, 1845", giving biographical and other information concerning the Park Village Community. The ex-novice, whose account of the Sisterhood as she knew it between 1850 and 1856 has already been quoted (pp. 37–8 above), reproduced as an appendix to *Five Years in a Protestant Sisterhood* the respective Rules for Orphans of the Park Village Community and the Roman Catholic Sisters of Mercy, in parallel columns. Barring some important changes and omissions in the Park Village regulations, the two codes are identical. Either the writer of the Ascot memorandum was in error about Port Royal or the Port Royal regulations had been superseded by 1850 by the rules of the Sisters of Mercy. There was certainly a flavour of Jansenist rigorism in the effort, reported as a "simple absurdity" by Mr Dodsworth, to enforce a rule of silence on "the poor orphans"—a "mischievous piece of extravagance" which was "soon set right".

of the school were amenable to the discipline of having no sugar with
their daily ration of rice and milk as a punishment for misbehaviour.
The older boys and girls required rougher treatment. The ex-novice
already quoted described one of the members of the household as a
"very tall, angular, good-natured, uneducated Scotch lady, who
thrashed the boys . . . scolded the girls". This lady—she is not
designated a Sister—has not been identified. But there is a small notebook in the archives at Ascot containing memoranda about Miss
Kebbel, in which her brief novitiate in the Regent's Park Community
is noted as having been distinguished not only by her exemplary
observance of Rule but also by the fact that she "had subdued the big
rough boys" of the Ragged School.

The care of orphans and the shelter of distressed women were not
the only corporal works of mercy undertaken by the Sisters. "Relief",
usually in the form of food, was given (in most cases by Mother
Emma in person) to "travellers" who applied for charity.

APPENDED NOTE TO CHAPTER FOUR

"THE RULES OF THE OUT-DOOR SCHOOL"

Sister Margaret Esther, c.s.j.b., during the time when she was an Assoc-
iate Sister of the Holy Cross (1850–1856) made copious notes of the
Rules and personnel of the Park Village Community. These memo-
randa are contained in a leather-bound locked book recently found at
Clewer. Among the several rules are the regulations for the Associate
Sisters, referred to above (p. 47), and "Rules of the Out-Door
School"—usually known as the "Ragged School" or "Poor School".
The former Rule is summarized at the end of Appendix 2 (p. 146).
The "Rules of the Out-Door School" direct that "boys shall be
eligible at four years old, girls at six, having no infectious complaint,
and baptized or having parents consenting to their being baptized".
"Every member of the school was to be presented with a conduct
card . . . and, if a boy, with a cap, round pinafore [!], and a pocket-
handkerchief to wear [sic] in school and at church; if a girl, with a
pinafore and pocket handkerchief, and also, if her hair is cut short,
with a cap and bonnet, and with capes and shawls during the winter.
. . . The articles of clothing are not to be taken to the children's homes,
but carefully hung up or put away when they leave school."

"The children as they entered the school-room were to go to their respective place . . . making a bow or curtsey at the door as they entered. The Sisters and Orphans present then dressed them one by one." "Behaviour in church" was strictly regulated: "The children were not to be allowed to loll or swing their feet. The boys were to keep their arms crossed whilst sitting and the girls with their hands in their laps. Boys and girls were to kneel in an upright posture with their hands joined together. . . . They were to be encouraged to join in the responses . . . and . . . in the singing if they were able." The regulation entitled "Of Breakfast" provides "all the children who came to church in tolerable time should have breakfast afterwards of rice and milk and water and bread. . . . Any child notoriously restless or careless at church was to be deprived of sugar with the rice", as noted by Miss Cusack. "A piece of bread was to be given to each and a second piece, if they desired it, when they had finished eating their rice. . . . During the boys' breakfast one or two of the Sisters were to examine each child to discover whether it was clean[1] and neat and so deserving of the farthing which was awarded in case they came to school in time to be dressed for church."

Besides daily instruction in the Church Catechism and Christian faith and practice, the children were taught reading, spelling, writing, and "tables". Instruction was given in singing, "so far as to help them in chanting and singing at church and amusing themselves with innocent little songs at home". The girls were to be taught needle-work and knitting, and the boys arithmetic, geography, and history. Arrangements were provided for holidays at Christmas, Easter, and Whitsuntide, as also three weeks during the summer. The other feasts of the Church were to be holidays.

Among the directions for "Punishment and Discipline" was the quaint provision that "a cane should be kept at hand to admonish the children and to enforce obedience and a sharp touch might be given at the moment when a child exhibited any decided impertinence or defied an injunction, as to keep silence, always assuming that it could be done without anger or perturbation. . . . Reiterated strokes must not be given on any occasion. The cane should not be used so much as an instrument of correction, but rather as a sign and assistance in gaining the attention and promptitude of obedience."

The direction that "a child who told a lie wilfully to deceive should

[1] Particular attention had to be given to the condition of the children's heads.

go down to the bottom of the class" was accompanied by the provision that "a child should not be considered to have wilfully told a lie when he promptly denied a sudden accusation; he should rather be checked for answering without giving himself time to think". The children were to be "often reminded to go straight home and not to stay in the streets to play till they had leave from their parents"—a regulation of particular importance in a neighbourhood such as that in which the children lived who attended the "Ragged School".[1] Noteworthy is the direction that it "would be better in general to pass over any faults than to make enquiries amongst the children or to risk charging a child unjustly or on an uncertainty".

---

[1] It has been impossible to identify the site of the "Ragged School". All that is known is that it was situated in "one of the worst parts of the district".

5

"Our Devonport Sisters"

AUTUMN AND WINTER
1848

In her letter of St Matthew's Day 1848, quoted in the preceding chapter, Sister Jane wrote to her sister:

> We have had such a pleasant visit just lately from our two Devonport
> —Sisters, one must call them, though they do not belong to our Sister-
> hood, except that we are all one. . . . Please God, they are going to begin
> a Sisterhood [in Devonport], and they have the Bishop's warm sanction
> and blessing. One chief object of their Sisterhood is to receive the orphans
> of the seamen. It is to be called "The Orphans' Home". . . . The senior[1]
> of them has been having a very large class of boys of an evening after
> their dockyard work: and this is to go on. . . . The Bishop has promised
> them daily service and weekly communion. . . . It is so blessed to begin
> with the Bishop's sanction: they have more in this respect than we. . . .
> I hope we may have our Bishop's in time, please God. We have only a
> negative sanction at present.

The "Devonport Sisters" were Miss Priscilla Lydia Sellon and Miss Catherine Elizabeth Chambers. Miss Sellon was an elder daughter of Commander William Richard Baker Sellon (late Smith), R.N., retired, of Part-y-Seal, near Grosmont, on the border of Hereford-shire and Monmouthshire. Miss Chambers was the daughter of one of Commander Sellon's brother officers, Commander David Chambers, R.N., of Oakley Hall, Bucks. Her older brother, Mr John David Chambers, was a rising young barrister, recently appointed Recorder of Salisbury, who in 1845 had come with his wife, the Hon. Henrietta Laura Wodehouse, to live in Regent's Park. Mr Chambers was Vicar's Warden at Christ Church, Albany Street. His association with the leaders of the Catholic Revival in the Church of England

---

[1] If seniority in age was intended by this word, as it doubtless was, Sister Jane was in error, since the young lady referred to was of the same age as her companion.

and his conviction of the soundness of that Church's claim to the liturgical and devotional, as well as the doctrinal, heritage of her past, gave him a sympathetic and practical interest in the revival of the Religious Life which was taking place in the parish of which he was a Warden. It was in Mr Chambers' house in Cumberland Terrace that Miss Sellon was given an opportunity to lay before a party of clergy and laymen her plans for relieving the spiritual and moral destitution, as well as the ignorance and material poverty, of the slums of the "Three Towns" of Devonport, Stonehouse, and Plymouth.

Mrs Chambers has left an account of this meeting:

> We were in the habit of receiving Miss Sellon at our house in the Regent's Park (my husband's sister was the first to join her Community). Soon after the Bishop of Exeter had asked her to work in Plymouth, we had a small party to meet her, of friends much interested in her proposed under-taking ... Miss Sellon sat in the middle of the room and with great modesty and diffidence gave an account of what she proposed to do. She had no personal attractions, but was very pleasant in manner. She often repeated her visits.

One important and immediate result of Miss Sellon's visits to her friends in Cumberland Terrace was the decision of Mr Chambers' sister, Catherine, to dedicate herself to the proposed venture for God and for souls in the Three Towns. Catherine Elizabeth Chambers, at the age of twenty-seven—the same age as Miss Sellon—was a young woman of "extraordinary beauty", "tall and graceful" (in contrast to Miss Sellon's short stature), and like Miss Sellon endowed with a "most winning manner".

It was probably during one of the aforementioned visits in the home of Mr and Mrs Chambers that another event took place, of far-reaching import to the revival of the Religious Life and to the history of the Sisterhood already established. This was the introduction of Miss Sellon to Dr Pusey, soon after she had responded to the challenge of Henry Phillpotts, Bishop of Exeter, to "the Christian charity of England" for assistance in meeting the "accumulation of spiritual wants" of the ignorant poverty-stricken inhabitants of what the Bishop declared to be "the most densely crowded" area in England.[1]

[1] Mother Bertha Turnbull, Miss Sellon's successor as Superior of the Society founded by Miss Sellon, writing to Canon Liddon in 1883, stated her belief that Miss Sellon knew Dr Pusey before her visit to Regent's Park following her decision to respond to Bishop Phillpotts' appeal.

The Priory of Jesus Christ, Ascot, in 1862

The Priory of Jesus Christ, Ascot, in 1964

The Bishop's appeal was published in *The Guardian* of 5 January 1848. It did not come to Miss Sellon's attention until the early Spring when she was on the point of leaving England to recuperate from her first serious illness in the milder climate of Italy.[1] To the daughter of a sailor the Bishop's challenge came with particular appeal as affecting the welfare of the hundreds of sailors' families inhabiting a seaport town. Miss Sellon's reaction to the Bishop's plea was the first of many instances in which she exerted the power of will and nervous energy which has for generations distinguished members of the Sellon family, enabling them under stress of emergency or critical need so completely to ignore bodily weakness as to execute with efficiency and vigour enterprises which would tax the powers of far more robust constitutions. Ignoring frail health and foregoing Italy, with her father's approval Miss Sellon sought an interview with the Bishop of Exeter, to place herself and her fortune at his service in meeting in such measure as she might be able the religious, educational, and social needs of the people—in particular the boys and girls—of the Devonport slums. The proposal of a young gentlewoman still in her twenties not only to work, but to live day and night, among these wretched folk might well have drawn from a Victorian Tory prelate a shocked refusal of her offer. But the redoubtable Henry of Exeter, apparently without hesitation, gave his "sanction and blessing" to Miss Sellon's undertaking. Armed with her father's consent and the Bishop's blessing, she went at once to Devonport to gain at first hand a notion of the problems which would challenge her.

By April Miss Sellon's plans were so far determined that she was ready to go up to London to lay them before her friends there, and to seek their counsel. On her return to Devonport she was accompanied by Miss Chambers. The increased efficiency which resulted from even so slight an increase in the numbers of workers confirmed Miss Sellon in whatever aspiration she may have previously entertained of establishing a Sisterhood. Without dedicated communal

---

[1] Madeira is named as Miss Sellon's destination in the *History of St Dunstan's Abbey School, 1848–1928*, compiled by Sister Margaret Teresa, C.S.M.V., p. 9. This error (as it has been proved to be by the letter of Dr Pusey, cited below) was perpetuated in *Priscilla Lydia Sellon*, whence it was adopted by Mr Peter F. Anson in *The Call of the Cloister*, p. 261. Since *Priscilla Lydia Sellon* was published in 1950, Mr A. W. Campbell discovered in the library of Pusey House, Oxford, the complete text of Dr Pusey's letter to the Reverend E. C. Coleridge, quoted in part by Canon Liddon in Volume III of his *Life of E. B. Pusey*, p. 193. In this letter Dr Pusey names Italy as Miss Sellon's proposed destination.

F

organization little could be accomplished of a stable character. It was
no doubt this conviction which led her, during convalescence from
an illness which had for a time interrupted her activities in the Three
Towns, to pay a visit in September to Dr Pusey at his home at Christ
Church, Oxford. Another guest of Dr Pusey at this time was Miss
Hughes, who had spent the early part of the Summer at No. 17 Park
Village West. Miss Hughes, as well as Dr Pusey, had valuable suggestions to make about the ordering of a Sisterhood. She also designed
and made the habit which Miss Sellon would eventually wear. From
Oxford Miss Sellon went with Miss Chambers, at Dr Pusey's invita-
tion, to Park Village West for the visit reported by Sister Jane Ellacombe, "to see what a Sisterhood was like".

There seems reason to believe that Dr Pusey hoped—perhaps
suggested—that Miss Sellon and Miss Chambers would join the already established Community, to carry on the work in Devonport as
Sisters of the Holy Cross. The visit to Park Village West did not,
however, produce the result supposedly hoped for by Dr Pusey. Miss
Sellon was repelled by the constraint and aloofness of the Sisters,
which she attributed to a Rule unsuited to women whose life, for the
immediate future at least, must be one of varied external activities
during seven or eight of the twenty-four hours of a day, and of
friendly contact with their neighbours. It was this experience, no
doubt, which led her to the decision "not to join the Community at
Park Village, but to form another, of which she should herself be
Superior, for work among the poor of Devonport".

Although the Rule of the Sisterhood of the Holy Cross was not
adopted by the new Society, certain of its provisions were incorporated
in the tentative directions for the ordering of the daily life of the
Sisters sanctioned by Bishop Phillpotts when he accepted the office of
Episcopal Visitor. A copy of the Park Village Admission Service was
sent to Devonport for use at the reception as Sisters of Mercy of
Priscilla Lydia Sellon and Catherine Elizabeth Chambers. The service
was held on 27 October 1848, the Eve of the Feast of St Simon and St
Jude, preceding the First Vespers of the Feast. Dr Pusey is supposed
to have been present and to have officiated. Although, as in the older
Community, no vows were required or made publicly, those of the
Sisters who wished to bind themselves to life-long Poverty, Chastity,
and Obedience, "made the three vows" each in her own heart.

So was formally and officially inaugurated "The Church of England Society of Sisters of Mercy of Devonport and Plymouth", with Priscilla Lydia Sellon as "Lady Superior" and Henry Phillpotts Bishop of Exeter, as Visitor. The Sisters were invested with the simple but "sufficiently distinctive" habit of black serge, designed and made by Miss Marian Hughes. Later in the year, when Bishop Phillpotts visited the Three Towns to administer Confirmation, the two Sisters presented themselves to him for his formal blessing as Sisters of Mercy. This blessing they always reckoned as their "Consecration[1] ... a seal on the inward devotion of their whole being to God".

[1] "Consecration", rather than "Profession", is the word used by Mother Lydia in her reference to this blessing by the Bishop in her *Reply* to the attack made on her and her Society of the Reverend James Spurrell in 1852. The word was chosen, it may be supposed, as being more "primitive" than "Profession". It is the word used in the Pontifical—to wit, "The Consecration of a Virgin"—which was the service used at the Profession of Miss Marian Hughes in 1841. On it was based the Admission Service of the Sisterhood of the Holy Cross, a form of which, as noted above, was used at the reception as Sisters of Mother Lydia and her companion. It was perhaps the use of the word "consecration" by Miss Sellon in her *Reply* to Mr Spurrell which suggested to Bishop Phillpotts his suspicion that the Lady Superior of Devonport and Plymouth attached to the word a connotation of an apostolic or semiepiscopal commission imparted to her as "Spiritual Mother" of the Sisters—a title to which Bishop Phillpotts expressed particular objection in his "Letter to Miss Sellon" of 28 March, 1852, summarized in *Priscilla Lydia Sellon*.

6

Sponsa Christi
1849—1850

Three personal ties bound the older Community in London to the new foundation in Devonport. One bond was the close association of Dr Pusey with both Communities—with London, as the formally acknowledged "Spiritual Superintendent"; with Devonport, by virtue of his unofficial personal relationship to its Superior as her loyal supporter and trusted adviser. The second point of contact was afforded by Miss Sellon's repetition from time to time of her earlier visit to the home of Mr and Mrs Chambers. It was not until the summer of 1849 that there was added the third bond—active participation by members of both Communities in a common work.

In June 1849, on the Feast of St Peter, Mother Emma Langston and Sister Katherine Ogilvie, with perhaps other Sisters, made formal Profession of the three Vows of Religion. Dr Pusey received their vows.[1] It was these two Sisters who, with Sister Sarah Anne Terrot, were sent by Dr Pusey to Plymouth in July at the urgent request of the Devonport Superior to help in nursing the victims of the cholera epidemic which was devastating the Three Towns. The Park Village Sisters who did not go to Plymouth "had the same kind [of sickness] to attend to, but it did not spread". Miss Hughes came with several

[1] Miss Cusack, in *Five Years* (p. 55), records that "on St Peter's Day, 1849 . . . [the] Superioress of a Sisterhood under [Dr Pusey's] care made [the three vows] to him". Mother Annie Louisa, c.s.m.v., in the account of Sister Katherine Ogilvie already cited (p. xi above), states that Sister Katherine "died after her Profession", which she relates to her nursing during the cholera (erroneously dated in 1848, instead of 1849). Sister Clara noted in her reminiscences that Sister Katherine was one of the three Sisters sent by Dr Pusey to Plymouth in 1849 to help Miss Sellon and her Sisters with the nursing. A memorandum preserved at Ascot Priory indicates that the third Sister sent from London to Plymouth was Sister Sarah Anne Terrot, correcting the impression, based on other statements, that Sister Sarah Anne joined Mother Lydia and her associates in forming the Devonport Society in 1848.

66

ladies from Oxford who hoped to join her in forming a Sisterhood there. They too had been sent by Dr Pusey to help in the overwhelming task undertaken by the Devonport Mother and her Sisters.

The story of that heroic work has been told in considerable detail by the late A. Clifton Kelway in *George Rundle Prynne* (pp. 48–60), and, with additional details derived from letters of one of the nurses (who later became a Sister) to members of her family, in *Priscilla Lydia Sellon*. Outstanding for selfless devotion and fearlessness in a company where all were selfless and unafraid was Sister Sarah Anne. Her health broke for a short time, but she was soon back at her gruesome task of laying out the dead.

Mother Lydia was ordered to bed by her physician, but did not remain there. She was on call day and night for duty—now in Plymouth and again, perhaps in the same night, in Devonport or Stonehouse. An elderly volunteer helper, Miss Amelia Warren, and a young Novice, who had been isolated with the orphans from danger of infection, were the only members of the Sisters' household who contracted cholera. Miss Warren recovered, to live twenty years longer to an honoured old age as a Sister of the Devonport Society, which she joined at the end of 1849. Novice Octavia Maillardet died, attended in her last hours by Mr Prynne, who gave her Holy Communion, and by Sister Sarah Anne. The Lady Superior never recovered fully from the effects of her defiance of the doctor's orders. Sister Katherine's health, already impaired by a severe fast during the previous Lent, broke down entirely after her return in the late autumn to Park Village West. Sister Sarah Anne remained in Plymouth as a member of the Devonport Society, finding the life there at that period more congenial than the stiffness of Park Village.

The beginning of Lent 1850 found Sister Katherine so far from complete recovery that Mother Emma was loath to sanction a repetition of the heroic fasting of the previous year: no food except a dish of thick oatmeal taken after 9 o'clock in the evening. The fast had been originally undertaken in emulation of what she knew to be Dr Pusey's own practice—especially during the last three days of Holy Week. Dr Pusey never exacted, or even consciously suggested, severe physical austerities to the practice of his penitents. But he was, in the early days of inexperience, not unwilling to sanction extraordinary mortifications voluntarily undertaken by his spiritual children. Of the case of Sister Katherine he wrote in later years: "Formerly we had to learn through experience the effect of fasting. . . . That dear good Sister Katherine. . . . I let [practice], or perhaps mentioned to her, that long fast from Maundy Thursday to Easter Day."

As the result of her Lenten fast, Sister Katherine "at the beginning of Passion Week[1] . . . was much reduced; on Holy Thursday she took some porridge at noon, and from that time did not permit anything to pass her lips, not even a drop of water, until Easter Sunday". Then it was that Mother Emma, according to Dr Pusey's account, "gave her hard"—that is, solid—"food which brought on . . . gastric fever". The symptoms of the disease manifested themselves some ten days after Easter. Sister Katherine "never rose from her bed again". Gastric fever developed into what the Sister's death certificate diagnosed as "tubercular peritonitis". During the rest of Eastertide, Pentecost, and the first four weeks of the Trinity season she lingered, daily increasing in the sanctity for which she was so highly esteemed, "her one thought and desire, to live to God and be with Him. . . . Her last act was one of conformity to the will of God. By giving up her own [will] she was able to communicate on the morning before her death, and to make her last confession." It may have been at this time that she expressed a "desire and longing" to receive the sacrament of Holy Unction. Her desire was fostered, perhaps, by the Scottish Episcopalian traditions of her family—traditions including, among other "usages", the ministration of Holy Unction. There was, however, no bishop of the English Church at that time who was liturgically competent, or would be willing, to bless the Holy Oil or administer the long disused sacrament. But by the Providence of God, Sister Katherine's relative, the Right Reverend Alexander Penrose Forbes, Bishop of the Scottish diocese of Brechin, was at Oxford at this time on a visit to Dr Pusey. Bishop Forbes was a zealous advocate not only of the revival of the Religious Life but also of the restoration to the Anglican Communion of the sacrament which his kinswoman wished to receive—"the lost Pleiad of the Anglican firmament" he later called it. He probably accompanied Dr Pusey to London when the latter was summoned to attend Sister Katherine in her last hours. There can be, therefore, no doubt that Bishop Forbes was the "very High Church bishop" who is said by

[1] In Tractarian and even later times Holy Week was called Passion Week. Holy Week is meant in the account given by Miss Goodman (*Sisterhoods in the Church of England*, p. 12) which is quoted in the text.

Miss Cusack to have administered the sacrament to Sister Katherine—
the first recorded ministration of Holy Unction, in the Church of
England, outside Non-Juring circles, since the reign of Edward VI.[1]

Sister Katherine's brother. Dr George Ogilvie (later Ogilvie-
Forbes) came to visit her in her illness, bringing with him a younger
sister, Rebecca,[2] who remained in London until her sister's death.
After receiving the sacraments Sister Katherine experienced such
marked relief from pain that she said that "she thought the Sisters
must have prayed for her pain to cease. . . . She begged [Dr Pusey] to
ask them not [to do so], as she did not wish to suffer one pain less
than was the will of God". She died at 10 o'clock in the evening of 27
June 1850.

"Dr Pusey arranged the funeral . . . to prevent the Sisters having
anxiety. He wrote a Latin inscription for her coffin, calling her
'Sponsa Christi'—the first probably in the Church of England since
the Reformation." Dr Pusey himself "read the Funeral Service. . . .
That over, he held a conference in which he spoke [to the Sisters] of
her high blessedness". "Nothing (he said) could be more beautiful
than the death of dear Sister Katherine. She panted for something
beyond her which she now has. . . . I have never known in her one
wish contrary to the will of God. And now that one of this Sisterhood is in Paradise, let us love one another more and more, and strive
by no thought . . . or word to displease your Lord."

A cloud of sorrow and bereavement still hung over the household
in Park Village West and Upper Albany Street when later in the
summer of 1850 a young Irish woman, Miss Margaret Anna Cusack,
herself not wholly recovered from the shock of her fiancé's sudden
and tragic death, came to the Sisterhood at the suggestion of Dr

[1] A rumour of this administration of Holy Unction must have reached hostile ears,
for in the same summer (1850) in which Sister Katherine was anointed, it was alleged
against the Reverend W. J. E. Bennet of St Barnabas', Pimlico, that he had administered
"Extreme Unction" to one of his parishioners at about the same time that Bishop Forbes
anointed Sister Katherine. Mr Bennet, however, denied that he had ever at any time
administered Holy Unction to anyone.

[2] Rebecca Forbes Ogilvie-Forbes was received as a Novice at Wantage in 1876.
She died before Profession. A niece of Sister Katherine, Helen Katherine Ogilvie-
Forbes, a daughter of Dr George Ogilvie-Forbes, joined the Society of St Margaret
of Scotland in 1882 and was known in Religion as Sister Katherine Mary. She was for
many years Superior of St Margaret's Convent, Aberdeen. A great-niece of Sister
Katherine of Park Village West is a Religious of the Sacred Heart. Another relative,
Dom David Ogilvie-Forbes, is a Monk of the English (Roman Catholic) Congregation
of the Order of St Benedict.

Pusey to make trial of her vocation. She was received on her arrival
by Mother Emma and Sister Jane with sincere, if somewhat constrained, cordiality. She was welcomed not only as a recruit to the
thinned ranks of the Community, but especially as being already one
of Dr Pusey's "children".

The aspirant's first two weeks were spent in what she was told was
a "retreat", preparatory to her reception as a Probationer or Novice.
In silence and in solitude in her cell, where her meals were brought
to her—without direction or guidance of any sort, and leaving her
cell only to attend Mattins and Evensong at Christ Church (no mention is made of the Offices in the Sisters' Oratory)—the "retreatant"
awaited the coming of Dr Pusey to invest her with the black serge
dress "with white at the neck" and the "girdled cap" of a Sister
Probationer. Into the life of the Sisterhood, described by her in a
passage already quoted, the new Probationer fitted happily, finding in
the work assigned to her in the Ragged School a congenial sphere for
the exercise of her love and compassion for the poor. For her Superior
she conceived an affection and regard which survived the storms that
eventually swept them both into the Roman Catholic Church. For
Dr Pusey also she had a reverent esteem, which she never ceased to
express, even when as a Roman Catholic she tempered her praise with
criticism of his ecclesiastical views and his conduct of the Sisterhood.
Dr Pusey was quoted as "speaking very kindly of her" to one of the
Sisters, noting in particular the sweetness of her disposition.[1]

[1] In 1889 Miss Cusack published, under her name as a Roman Catholic Religious,
Sister Mary Frances Clare Cusack, an autobiography entitled *The Nun of Kenmare*, in
which she gave a brief account of her life in the Sisterhood of the Holy Cross, noting
particularly her esteem for both Dr Pusey and Mother Emma Langston, but making
derogatory mention of Mother Lydia Sellon. On its publication, Dr Liddon wrote to
Sister Clara Powell asking for any information which she could give concerning Miss
Cusack, mentioning also the anonymous autobiography published in 1869 entitled *Five
Years in a Protestant Sisterhood and Ten Years in a Catholic Convent*. Sister Clara's
reply, dated 16 February, 1889, is preserved at Pusey House, Oxford. She wrote: "I
am only sorry that I can not furnish you with any incidents concerning Miss Casack
[*sic*] (Margaret Anna). She was only a young probationer during her stay at St Saviour's
and was not . . . under my charge. I also saw her when at Bristol we were both members of the Devonport Society. Indeed her stay in both (Communities] can only have
reached three years or so. [She was actually in the two Societies a total of some five years
(1850–5). T. J. W.] Mother Bertha is writing to one of our Plymouth Sisters, who
speaks of her, in order to learn any particulars she can, and will let you have them as
soon as possible. Our beloved Reverend Father spoke very kindly of Miss Casack [*sic*]
to Sister Georgiana, saying that 'she is very sweet'. . . . At present we know nothing
of the book published in 1869. As she had so little experience of English convents, I

hope it was not hers." The particulars learned by Mother Bertha from "one of the Plymouth Sisters" and (one may suppose) sent to Dr Liddon have not been found. In a letter addressed to Mother Eldress Catherine in 1854, Mother Emma gave the following estimate of Miss Cusack's character as a Novice in the Park Village Community: "As to dear Margaret Anna, she has proved a truly dutiful trustful child to me in yielding herself up to dearest Mother and she will have the reward of her loving obedience. I should so like to hear of her wearing the Devonport Novices' dress, until she can be really admitted as Mother's Child . . . Margaret Anna has been entirely and truly my child. I have known her as well as any one human being could know another, and have often been very anxious about her . . . She is superficial, apt to think that she knows more than she really does, and is often independent and inaccurate in what she says. She quickly gets buoyed up by success and beyond measure depressed when anything goes wrong. But she has been taking pains with herself in all these respects for two years past. But she greatly needs a loving watchful eye over her in her work and she is thankful for correction and admonition. She has often made me very anxious work, though no one could be more loving or repentant. She is most affectionate and loving, with great reverence and a great longing to be truly humble and obedient."

7

The First Convent since the Dissolution of the Monasteries 1850—1852

On the north-east corner of Osnaburgh Street and New Road (Euston Road of to-day) opposite the Church of the Holy Trinity, St Marylebone, in the Borough of St Pancras, there stood for many years previous to 1850 a group of buildings consisting of a dwelling facing Osnaburgh Street and two dwellings facing the New Road. The land on which these buildings stood was Crown Property, held on lease from "The Right Honourable Her Majesty's Commissioners of Woods, Forests, Land Revenues, Works, and Buildings". Ecclesiastically the land and buildings were situated in the newly constituted district of St Mary Magdalene, Munster Square. Previous efforts to secure a site for a permanent home for the Sisterhood of the Holy Cross having failed, negotiations were instituted and carried through for the taking over by "Clarissa Powell, of Park Village West, Spinster", of the lease of the land and for the purchase of the buildings standing thereon. The money for the purchase of the lease, in the sum of £2,600, was given by Miss Powell, who signified her intention of demolishing the buildings fronting on Osnaburgh Street for the purpose of erecting in the "Gothic or pointed style of architecture . . . or any other style . . . more agreeable to [the lessors]", a house for the residence of the lessee and of "other ladies who may be associated with her to the number of fourteen, and of forty orphan girls and fifteen women of the class of servants out of place who have no home—such orphan girls and women to be members of the Church of England and to be resident entirely and boarded in the said house and under the control and management and at the charge of the [lessee] and her companions". Drawings, "showing the architectural design, elevation of the same, and the plan and dimension of each floor"—the work of William Butterfield, furnished without cost—were submitted to the "Honourable Board" for their inspection. The plans had already been approved by the owner of the adjoining house, No. 2 Osnaburgh Street. The rent of the land was £100 a year.

The plans provided for a frontage on Osnaburgh Street comprising a parlour and refectory, a class-room, a waiting-room for the poor, kitchen, wash-house, laundry, with twelve cells for the Sisters, and a dormitory for twenty-five orphans; also a wing or "L" at right angles to the street frontage providing day-rooms for the orphans and "distressed women", respectively, as well as dormitories on the floor above for twenty additional orphans and fifteen more women. An extension of this wing into the garden behind the front buildings contained a common room for the Sisters, an infirmary, and additional sleeping quarters. At the east end of the "L", adjoining the garden extension, the chapel was to be built.

In addition to the £2,600 paid for the lease, Sister Clara contributed £2,900 towards the cost of the building. An additional sum of £3,277 was given by "friends of the Sisters", either directly or through Dr Pusey and Mr Upton Richards. Of the last named sum £200 was designated for the chapel. "The parent of a deceased Sister" (Mrs Ogilvie) made an offering of £100 for the chapel and an additional £100 for the "general fund". A final gift of £400 from the brother-in-law of the Hon. Miss Napier, Mr J. G. Hubbard, a wealthy merchant of the City of London and a Director of the Bank of England, the future Lord Addington and founder of St Alban's, Holborn, brought the amount available for building to £6,076. Sister Charlotte White had already made herself responsible for £100 a year to cover the annual rent.

Not waiting for the formal permission of the Crown Commissioners to proceed with building operations, Dr Pusey and the Sisters chose for the date of laying the foundation-stone 14 September, Holy Cross Day, the Feast of the Title of the Sisterhood and the fiftieth anniversary of the baptism of the Spiritual Superintendent. The ceremony was performed by Dr Pusey quietly and without previous public notice on Saturday 14 September, at 2 o'clock in the afternoon. The dedication of the Home was to the Holy Cross under the title of St Saviour.[1]

---

[1] The title, St Saviour, had been adopted by Dr Pusey in 1845 as a "code" for "Holy

The laying of the foundation-stone of the first Religious House erected as such since the Dissolution of the Monasteries in the sixteenth century was followed three weeks later in Plymouth by the laying of the foundation-stone of the second such "House of Religion". On 5 October 1850 the Bishop of Exeter, in virtue of his office of Visitor of the Devonport Society and "in behalf of the Church", laid the foundation-stone of a "House of Religion and Charity for the Sisters of Mercy" of that Society. Designed, like St Saviour's, by Mr Butterfield (likewise without fee), the Abbey, dedicated to St Dunstan, was to occupy the site of the Sisters' cholera hospital in the Five Fields overlooking the Mere (now Victoria Park), where in 1849 at a temporary altar erected in the main ward the daily celebration of the Holy Eucharist was restored to the Anglican Communion.[1] A description of the Abbey buildings and an account of the laying of the corner-stone and of the disgraceful demonstration which ensued are given in *Priscilla Lydia Sellon*.

The quietness, amounting to secrecy, with which Dr Pusey had laid the corner-stone of St Saviour's in Osnaburgh Street, stands in sharp contrast to the official and public character of the ceremony performed by the Lord Bishop of Exeter in Plymouth. The Church papers, notably *The Guardian* and *The Churchman's Magazine*, published full accounts of the solemnity in the Five Fields.[2] Yet it was the unheralded, almost clandestine, beginning of conventual restoration in Regent's Park rather than the publicized building operations at Plymouth which attracted the notice of the Law. It is reported that the work in Osnaburgh Street was suspended until the legality of erecting a conventual house, provided it was not for the use of Roman Catholic Religious, was established by the findings—or the rulings—of a Parliamentary Committee.[3] In consequence of this delay the

---

Cross", when the Bishop of Ripon objected to the latter dedication for the votive church erected by Dr Pusey in Leeds and consecrated in 1845.

[1] The site of this altar is marked by brass plate in one of the rooms of St Dunstan's Abbey School.

[2] Printed and bound copies of *The Order of Service to be Used in Laying the Foundation Stone of the House of Religion and Charity for the Sisters of Mercy of Devonport and Plymouth by the Lord Bishop of Exeter, October 5th, The Year of our LORD MDCCCL*, were provided. One of these bound and printed copies, along with the original draft in the handwriting of Mother Lydia, is stored in the Coffer now kept in the Sacristy of the Priory Church of Jesus Christ, Ascot.

[3] Miss Goodman, in *Sisterhoods in the Church of England* (Preface to the Second Edition, p. vi) stated that "building operations were for some time suspended, because

Sisters were not able to occupy their new home until Michaelmas 1852—the fifth anniversary of the reception as a Sister of the donor of the site, Sister Clara.

The plans for St Saviour's, it will be remembered, provided accommodation for fourteen Sisters. Between the Wednesday in Easter Week 1845, when the first two Sisters went into residence at No. 17 Park Village West, and Michaelmas 1852, some eighteen women had been received as Sisters or admitted as aspirants or "Probationers". Of that number nine had left the Sisterhood: Miss Bruce, on account of ill health; Miss Napier, temporarily, to discharge a filial obligation; Miss Benett and Miss Ind, under pressure of parental opposition. Mr Upton Richards' aspirant, Sister Harriet Barraud was in 1851 at Devonport (where she was known as Sister Maude) and later "among the Sisters" of the nascent Society of All Saints in Mortimer Street, London. Sister Susanna Logan, like her Scottish compatriot, Sister Sarah Anne Terrot, had joined the Devonport Society in 1849. Three—Miss Wilcox, Miss Colt, and Miss White—had been received into the Roman Catholic Church. One, Sister Katherine Ogilvie, had died. The Sisters who went into residence at St Saviour's in September 1852 were, so far as is known at present, Mother Emma, Sister Jane, Sister Etheldreda, Sister Clara, the Probationer, Margaret Anna Cusack, and probably Sister Caroline Paul, whose name is given in the Census Return for No. 17 Park Village West, of April 1851, as of a Sister of Mercy there resident. Of this lady nothing is known beyond the data furnished by the Census Return: her name, her place of birth, Exeter; her age, thirty-seven years; and her status as unmarried and a Sister of Mercy. If this Sister

---

the Government was not able to decide whether Religious Houses were in accordance with the genius of English Law; ultimately, however, the Legislature suffered the work to proceed". Cf. *Report of the Select Committee on Conventual and Monastic Institutions* (1871), to the effect that "members of the Church of England, of the Greek Church, or any other Church than the Church of Rome, are perfectly free to take monastic vows, to enroll themselves in communities of conventual or monastic character, and to found and endow institutions of that kind without any restrictions and subject only to the general rules which govern the disposition of private property in the hands of individuals". Inasmuch as recent research, including examination of Parliamentary Reports for the years 1850, 1851, and 1852, has failed to discover record or mention of the procedure indicated by Miss Goodman, it has been surmised that the latter's reference is to a possible objection on the part of the Commissioners Woods and Forests to the beginning of building operations before formal permission to proceed had been asked or granted.

Caroline Paul was still in the Community when the Sisters moved to Osnaburgh Street, the number of Sisters would be six. It is possible that Associate Sister Margaret Hooper (in later years a Sister at Clewer) was a seventh member of the Regent's Park Community at this time.

The Sisterhood of the Holy Cross had not realized the hopes of Dr Pusey expressed in his letters to Miss Hughes and other interested friends in the earlier days. Yet the venture in Park Village West had not been barren of the fruit for which Dr Pusey expressed bright hopes, although it grew and ripened elsewhere than in Regent's Park. In 1848, the year of Miss Sellon's foundation in Devonport, a young Berkshire parson, the Reverend William John Butler, recently appointed vicar of Wantage, laid the foundation of what was destined to become the largest of Anglican Sisterhoods, the Community of St Mary the Virgin. In the same year the Nursing Sisterhood of St John's House was inaugurated in London. In 1849 Miss Hughes was free, at last, to realize her aspiration to live in community the life to which she had dedicated herself in 1841, and to found in Oxford, in December 1849, the Society of the Holy and Undivided Trinity. At Clewer, a suburb of Windsor, the rector, the Reverend Thomas Thellusson Carter, with the capable and devoted collaboration of a widowed cousin of Novice Margaret Anna Cusack, the Hon. Harriet Monsell, inaugurated in November 1852 the Community of St John Baptist. In the previous year, 1851, Miss Harriet Brownlow Byron, a parishioner and penitent of Mr Upton Richards of Margaret Street, who had been a visitor at No. 17 Park Village West when her friend, Miss Ethel Benett, was there "among the Sisters", took the first steps towards the establishment of the Society of the All Saints Sisters of the Poor. By Michaelmas, 1852, when the six or seven Sisters from Park Village West took up residence in Osnaburgh Street, the little stream of conventual life which had risen in Regent's Park seven years before had become a river.

APPENDED NOTE TO CHAPTER SEVEN

St Saviour's Home, as related in Chapter 13, was sold to Mr E. H. Palmer in 1877 and became a hospital for the treatment of cancer under the direction of his wife. After her death it passed successively into the hands of the All Saints' Sisters of the Poor, the Sisters of the Epiphany, and the Community of the Presentation. The building was demolished in 1964 to make room for the widening of Euston Road and the redevelopment of the area eastwards to Tottenham Court Road.

8

Secession—Abduction—Rescue
1851—1852

During the two years which passed between the laying of the foundation stones of the first two Religious Houses of the Anglican Revival and their occupation by the respective Sisterhoods for which they were built, less happy events had occurred affecting one or both of these Communities. The controversy over the Church of England's doctrine of Holy Baptism, aggravated by the Judgement of the Privy Council, a purely secular body, in the Gorham Case, had disastrous effects throughout the Church. Those effects were nowhere more marked than at Christ Church, Albany Street, notably among the Sisters who attended its services and listened to the sermons preached by the vicar. In the Spring of 1850 Mr Dodsworth began to doubt the validity of the claim of the Church of England to be the Catholic Church of the land. The willingness of the two Archbishops and of most of the Bishops to admit the right, claimed in the Judgement of the Privy Council, of an individual clergyman to "play fast and loose" with the doctrine of Holy Baptism as set forth in the Book of Common Prayer, was shocking enough. But when the State claimed the right, and many of the leaders of the Church allowed the claim, to settle questions of doctrine, Mr Dodsworth and others of both clergy and laity were finally convinced that they had been in error regarding the true character of the Established Church, and that their salvation was imperilled by their remaining in her communion. Mr Dodsworth did not confine the expression of his unsettled state of mind to clerical gatherings or letters to the Church press. He considered it to be his duty to take his parishioners with him, step by step, along the way of doubt and final disillusionment. His sermons, Dr Pusey reported to Mr Keble, "communicated this unsettlement to the members of the congregation, particularly to the Sisters."

78

"What shall I do", Dr Pusey asked Mr Keble, "if Dodsworth continues this sort of sermon? My children at the Sisterhood were so distressed at the last about Balaam, and the appeal to the young to act and think for themselves, that the Mother begged not to go there again. I suggested that they try one more Sunday: but what if these sermons continue? One would not wish them to stay at home, and to pass Christ Church would be very painful." Mr Keble replied that he wished that the Sisters could stop their ears and read their Bibles during the sermon. It would be the best thing. "I fear", he added, "they can not all be depended on for doing it. In so many there would probably be some who would not or could not do it." He wondered if it would be wrong to make a distinction and let them stay who might be trusted not to attend to the sermon, while others were kept at home, or went somewhere else? "I really don't see", he concluded, "that for a sort of punctilio, any should be allowed to stay and get unsettled."

What action was taken is not recorded. But it is certain that the Sisters heard enough, and some were sufficiently moved by what they heard, to allow themselves to be drawn along the way along which Mr Dodsworth was rapidly moving. One of Dr Pusey's "children" was so affected—Sister Jane Ellacombe. A visit which, for reasons of health, she had been permitted to pay to an uncle in 1850, did her "a good deal of harm" by causing her "to feel that what was believed . . . commonly in the Church [of England] was so different from what [the Tractarians] believed that they were not honest members of the Church of England". She was exceedingly shaken, Dr Pusey informed Mr Keble in a letter written in February 1851, in which he suggested that he and Mr Keble "throw cold water" on a plan then being considered for a similar visit to relatives early in 1851.

Another of Dr Pusey's "children" who had been likewise "shaken" was Sister Clara Powell. Mr Dodsworth's spiritual child, Sister Charlotte White, was well on the way towards fulfilling Mr Dodsworth's prognostication when Miss Colt left the Anglican fold, that Miss White "might be", like Miss Colt, "a sort of black sheep in the flock". Dr Pusey's arguments were sufficiently convincing to keep the theologically minded Sister Jane, the student of Pearson *On the Creed*, from leaving the Church of her Baptism. Sister Clara also seemed to be satisfied.

Not so Sister Charlotte. When in January 1851 Mr Dodsworth

G

was received into the Roman Catholic Church, Miss White, with several members of the congregation of Christ Church, accompanied or followed him into the Roman Communion. Miss White took with her two of the orphans. As a matter of conscience she discontinued her contribution of £100 a year towards the support of the Orphans' Home, as also her annual gift of £100 to the Community funds and the £50 a year for the relief of the poor of Christ Church congregation.[1]

Dr Pusey's patient analysis and refutation of the points urged against the Catholic claims of the Church of England, to which he devoted much time in correspondence as well as conversation with Sister Clara, had succeeded in quieting her doubts, when Miss White took action to insure that her former companion in Religion should have first-hand knowledge of Roman Catholicism before she herself left England to enter a Carmelite Monastery in Paris. By the middle of September her plans were matured. The actual facts, stripped of the exaggerations and misrepresentations of Miss Goodman and Miss Cusack, and the equally false impression conveyed in Miss White's own letters, are given in the published statements of Commander Sellon, of Sister Clara herself, and of her mother. An effort has been made below, as in the briefer account given in *Priscilla Lydia Sellon*, to adhere strictly to those facts.

Sister Clara's movements were "watched for days and weeks together" before an opportunity was found to put Miss White's plans into operation. Early in the morning of 18 September 1851 Sister Clara, in company with one of the orphans, was on her way to Osnaburgh Street, when she was surprised and dismayed at seeing Miss White "standing before her on the pavement . . . holding on high

[1] In the course of attacks directed against Dr Pusey and the Sisterhoods with which he was associated by an eccentric Master of Eton, the Reverend W. G. Cookesley, in 1852, the allegation was made that when Miss White left the Sisterhood she had been mulcted (inferentially by Dr Pusey) of her entire fortune. Dr Pusey's categorical rebuttal of this charge in a letter published in *The Guardian* of 7 September 1853 (p. 593) is substantiated by the fact that Miss White, before leaving England in 1852 to join Carmel at the Monastery in the Rue d'Enfer in Paris, endowed at a cost of £15,000 St Anne's School in Little Albany Street, Regent's Park, as a thankoffering for her conversion to the Roman Catholic Church. (*Life of Cornelia Connelly*, p. 214, and *Memorials of Mr Serjeant Bellasis*, p. 101.) A further (anonymous) thank-offering of £10,000 was placed by her in the alms-box of the Oratory in King William Street, Strand, as purchase money for the site of projected Oratory Church in Brompton. Miss White, known in Carmel as Sister Mary Theresa of St Philip, died at the monastery in Paris on 3 February 1892.

a large crucifix", blocking her way. Sister Clara, seeking to escape from the importunities of her friend "to go to see a priest", turned to go in another direction. "But whichever way she turned, Miss White with great agility managed to place the crucifix in her path." At length seeing a cab draw up nearby, Sister Clara, not suspecting collusion, stepped into it. Before she could give the driver directions, Miss White joined her and ordered the cabman to take them to a Roman Catholic convent in Kensington. The orphan who had witnessed the kidnapping ran home in terror to Park Village West to tell Mother Emma that "Sister Charlotte had taken Sister Clara away in a cab". Mother Emma at once notified Mrs Powell, who was visiting friends in London, of the abduction of her daughter. The two mothers spent the rest of the day in fruitless search for the missing Sister. The next morning's post brought a letter from the convent in Kensington announcing Miss Powell's impending reception into the Roman Catholic Church.

At the convent in Kensington the prospective convert was received by the Mother Superior, who sent her at once, in company with Miss White, to the Oratory in King William Street, Strand. There "after several hours of vehement persuasion fortified by the threat of eternal damnation if she refused to submit", she was, in her own words, "terrified into submission to . . . conditional Baptism". When Mother Emma and Mrs Powell presented themselves the next morning at the Convent, they were informed that Miss Powell "was at church for her confession". When she returned, her mother "in great . . . distress and anger" demanded that she go back to Park Village West at once. With the help of Mother Emma, she was persuaded to consent to "see Dr Pusey". When her would-be co-religionists urged their new convert before leaving them to make a promise "to be faithful", Sister Clara, "naturally impulsive and affectionate", protested that she would be "firm in the faith". This protest Mother Emma was inclined to accept as an expression of genuine conviction, but Mrs Powell was insistent on her daughter's release from the convent, which was finally effected with the help of a police magistrate who lived nearby.

Dr Pusey, whose letters to Sister Clara written at this and other times[1] reveal a sympathetic understanding of her disposition and of

[1] Many of the *Spiritual Letters of Edward Bourverie Pusey* were addressed to Sister Clara between 1844 and the end of Dr Pusey's life: In Part I, Nos. XIII, XIV, XV,

her spiritual needs and capacities, was able to convince her that it was her duty to be faithful, not to her recent enforced allegiance, but to her experience of sacramental grace in the English Church and to her Religious Profession in the same. Back again in her old home, under the influence of her Superior and her spiritual guide, and with the encouragement of her own mother, Sister Clara was by the following Sunday "ready and desirous" to make public acknowledgement of her loyalty to the Church and Community of her first allegiance by receiving Holy Communion with the other Sisters in Christ Church.

Miss White in letters written at this time claimed that Sister Clara's return to Park Village West and the Church of England was an instance of what she designated "the mortal (?moral) slavery . . . which Dr Pusey brought his victims under, when he had them in his uncontrolled management". Sister Clara's movements were still watched by Miss White. When it was learned that she was expected to receive Holy Communion in Christ Church on the Sunday morning following her abduction and rescue, a spectacular effort by Miss White and her co-religionists to restrain their friend, by exercise of physical force, if necessary, from what they considered would be an act of sacrilegious apostasy, was made at the entrance of Christ Church when Sister Clara arrived in company with the households of Park Village West and Upper Albany Street. "She was assailed at the doors of the church with cries" from Miss White and her confederates, "who reproached her with being an apostate", calling on her "not to enter the building . . . lest by doing so . . . she bring down upon herself the most fearful condemnation. Ultimately a kind of struggle for her person took place", which ended in Sister Clara's rescue by her Anglican associates, two of whom succeeded in escorting her safely into the church. There she received Holy Communion in token of her loyalty to the Church of England. The failure of the unedifying demonstration in Albany Street did not cause Miss White to abandon hope that before the day arrived which had been appointed for Sister Clara's formal reception and First Communion in the Roman

XIX, XXI (?), XXII, XXIII, XXIV, XXV, XXVI, XXVII, XXVIII, XXIX, XXX, XXXI, XLII (?), XLIV, XLVI, XLVII, XLVIII (pp. 24–8; 34–79; 86–97); in Part II, Nos. IX, X, XI, XII, XIII (pp. 193–207), all written in 1851 in relation to the unsettlement of Sister Clara related in the text of this work. In Part IV, "Fragments of Conversations and Letters", "To One Distressed" (p. 297), "On Talking among Women" (p. 300), and many others, especially on pp. 338–44, were addressed to Sister Clara either by letter or word of mouth.

Catholic Church (24 September) she might be again rescued from Dr Pusey's "tyranny" and find freedom from "all scruple and doubtfulness" in the security of the Fold of Peter. Close watch was kept of Sister Clara's movements in the hope perhaps of waylaying her again and persuading her to recant her recantation. When the situation became intolerable, Dr Pusey suggested that the harrassed Sister take refuge with Mother Lydia, who would welcome her as a guest in her household in Plymouth. This was one of several instances of the Devonport Mother's kindness, noted by Sister Clara in an oblique reference to her own experience at this time, in receiving Sisters of the older Community, "if any needed to change their work" or were faced by other needs or problems. Accordingly, on 24 September, the day which had been appointed for her reception into the Roman Catholic Church, Sister Clara left London to join the Devonport-Plymouth household.

Sister Clara's stay in Plymouth met with the full approval of her mother, who visited her daughter on several occasions and found her happy and contented and full of gratitude to the Devonport Mother for her kindness. Mrs Powell consented to the publication in *The Guardian* of 24 November 1852, of a letter in which she emphatically denied the statement circulated by Miss White that her daughter's visit in Plymouth was shrouded in "painful mystery". Equally emphatic was Sister Clara's refutation of Miss White's inference that her "return" to the communion of the Church of England had been effected by Dr Pusey's "spiritual tyranny". To this denial she added the affirmation: "I am a faithful member of the Church of England and have no wish to leave her communion." Mrs Powell gave her consent to the publication of these statements in order to contradict the charges made by Miss White in letters written to a friend which (without Miss White's knowledge or consent) had made head-line publicity in the mid-nineteenth century counterpart of the "tabloids" of the twentieth—the "penny-a-liners". More convincing proof of Sister Clara's avowed loyalty to the Church of England are the fifty-two remaining years of her Religious Life lived in the odour of Anglican sanctity.

The publicity accorded to Sister Clara's abduction and alleged conversion did not follow immediately on the occurrence of that painful experience. It was not until the Autumn of the following year, 1852, that the public was apprised of the affair by the appearance, in the sensational "penny-a-liners", previously mentioned, of private letters of Miss White found on the person of a friend, an apostate from the Devonport Society. The Sisterhood of the Holy Cross had from the first shunned publicity and had until 1852 succeeded in remaining unknown outside a small circle. It was the publication of Miss White's letters in the Autumn of 1852 which drew the older Sisterhood into the unpleasant publicity which had begun again to harrass the Devonport Society.

Meanwhile the walls of both St Saviour's Home in Osnaburgh Street and St Dunstan's Abbey, Plymouth, were rising towards partial completion. Lack of funds delayed the full realization of Mr Butterfield's design for St Dunstan's.[1] In the case of St Saviour's the Sisters began residence in the partly finished convent as soon as accommodation was available for them and their charges. This was at Michaelmas 1852. The work of construction was not completed until 1853. It was after the Sisters went into residence at St Saviour's that Miss Mary Kebbel began her novitiate, accompanied to St Saviour's by Miss Caroline Augusta Madox, who hoped that she too might one day be received as a Sister. Miss Kebbel's novitiate, distinguished by her faithful observance of Rule and her ability to cope with the young ruffians of the Ragged School, was of brief duration —only four months. An account of this novitiate is given in the memorandum of Miss Kebbel's connection with Dr Pusey and the Sisterhood, preserved at Ascot Priory. Miss Kebbel first "went to see Dr Pusey in Park Village about 1847, but it was at Osnaburgh Street that she entered the Society and made her novitiate of four months. Then her father came up to town, and when Miss Langston (Mother Emma) saw his white hairs and heard about her mother, she said she could not keep Miss Kebbel: 'It would not be right.'" In later years Miss Kebbel thought that "she had no real vocation; she had joined

---

[1] When the Devonport Sisters began residence at the Abbey in 1852 only two units of the proposed building had been constructed. Another unit and an enclosing wall were added in the early 1860s. The cloister contemplated in the original plan was not added until recent years during the tenancy of St Dunstan's by the Sisters of St Mary the Virgin, Wantage. The proposed Abbey Church was never built. The fairly spacious refectory served as the Oratory during all the years of the occupation by the Devonport Society as also during the tenancy of the Wantage Sisters. When St Peter's Church was damaged by an incendiary bomb during the Second World War, this Oratory was used by the congregation of St Peter's Church for week-day services until the reconstruction of the church. One of the larger buildings—the one-time "House of Peace" —was used for the Sunday services.

[the Sisterhood] because Dr Pusey wished it. He had a way of making people do what he wished". Miss Kebbel described her room at St Saviour's as being "quite plainly furnished, with windows glazed. She stood on a table to see out . . . She worked in the Ragged School and Miss Langston was sorry to lose her, for she had subdued the big boys and kept her rule better than any of the other novices."[1] Miss Kebbel remained under the spiritual direction of Dr Pusey after her withdrawal from the Sisterhood, retaining her connection with the Sisters as an Associate of the Community. For many years she was a member of Dr Pusey's household in Oxford and helped the Sisters who tended him in his last illness in ministering to his spiritual comfort as well as to his physical needs.

When Sister Clara returned to Regent's Park from her visit in Plymouth she "brought back a heart devoted to Devonport" and the Devonport Superior—a devotion which she was at no pains to conceal. Miss Cusack, who was at that time resident in Park Village West, reported that after her return to London Sister Clara "could talk of little else but 'dearest Mother'[2]—her wonderful gifts, her self-sacrifices, her love for her spiritual children". The effect of this untactful praise of the character and rule of the Devonport Mother was to raise in the minds of some of the Sisters a suspicion that Dr Pusey would welcome, and Mother Lydia would not oppose, an arrangement by which the latter would assume control of the Sisterhood in Regent's Park.[3] The prospect of such an arrangement was viewed by some of the Sisters with favour: by others, with apprehension and dread. Among those who welcomed the prospect were Mother Emma and Sister Clara. The latter noted in her *Reminiscences* that "one at least" of the Sisters of the older Community whom Mother

[1] Miss Cusack made a like claim for herself in her autobiography, *The Story of My Life*: "Miss Langston . . . said often that I was the only Sister who never gave her any trouble, or who had any idea of obedience."

[2] This term, applied to Mother Lydia from the earliest days of the Society by the Sisters, was almost invariably used by Dr Pusey in his informal references to her whom in more formal reference he called "the Devonport Mother".

[3] In the memoranda prepared by Sister Clara for Dr Liddon, from which previous citations have been made, it is stated that "Dr Pusey had ever desired a union between the [two] Societies". The proposed assumption of control of the London Sisterhood by the Devonport Superior has been interpreted as a preliminary step towards realizing Dr Pusey's hope of eventually uniting all the Sisterhoods of the English Church into a single Order of which Mother Lydia would be the Superior General. (Cf. [Cusack] *Five Years, etc.*, p. 110; Cusack, *The Story of My Life*, p. 77; G. W. E. Russell, *Dr Pusey*, pp. 86–7.)

Lydia "kindly received" when they "needed to change their work for a time ... brought back a heart devoted to Devonport",[1] and that later, "one by one [other] hearts were drawn to Devonport". Of those who dreaded the change of Superiors, Sister Jane is specifically named by Miss Cusack, who was herself averse to the absorption of the Community to which she belonged. Eventually (in 1853) Mother Emma, without the knowledge of the Sisters, bound herself to Mother Lydia by a promise of personal and individual obedience.

Sister Clara did not remain long among the Sisters in Regent's Park. Her heart drew her back to the "Paradise" which she thought she had found in the Devonport Society. Apparently neither Dr Pusey nor Mother Lydia was averse to her change of allegiance. It was Dr Pusey who suggested her visit to Devonport. No doubt Mother Lydia welcomed her as a recruit for the Second Order of her Society which was being formed to meet the needs and aspirations of those called to the enclosed life of contemplatives. Probably the London Sisters were glad to be spared Sister Clara's *encomia* of the Devonport Society and its Superior. Although not formally received into the Devonport Society until 1854, Sister Clara spent most of her time in Plymouth.

[1] "I thought the Devonport Society was Paradise", Sister Clara told Miss Trench many years later.

9

Co-operation

On 22 April 1852, some six months before the Sisters of the Holy Cross moved from Park Village West and Upper Albany Street into their permanent home, the Church of St Mary Magdalene, situated at the corner of Osnaburgh Street and Munster Square, one block north of St Saviour's, was consecrated by the Bishop of London. The Reverend Edward Stuart, a former curate of Mr Dodsworth at Christ Church, had been appointed incumbent when the district of St Mary Magdalene's was formed. The foundation-stone of the new church had been laid in 1849 by Baron Alderson, one of the Wardens of Christ Church, "after a procession through the streets, astonishing to the neighbourhood at that time". Since the new church was nearer to St Saviour's than Christ Church, St Mary Magdalene's became the Sisters' place of worship, although they continued their ministrations among the poor of Christ Church under the direction of Mr Dodsworth's successor, the Reverend H. W. Burrows.

Mr Stuart was one of the younger disciples of the Tractarian Revival who recognized that Catholic doctrine could be most effectively taught to the simple folk whom they were trying to win for the Church by the interpretative symbolism of Catholic worship. The services of the new church presented as marked a contrast to the restrained ceremonial of Christ Church as did its Gothic architecture to the classical style of the older building. St Mary Magdalene's was one of the first churches of the Catholic Revival to restore the ceremonial use of incense to parish worship. The occasion of its introduction was the Midnight Mass of Christmas 1854. Since the Mass was immediately preceded by Solemn Mattins and Procession at 10.30 or 11.00 p.m. of what was still Christmas Eve, the Sisters from

St Saviour's, who made their communions at the Mass were in doubt as to whether they should receive the Sacrament at the "early Cele-bration" on Christmas morning.[1]

The Regent's Park Community was scarcely mentioned in the earlier manifestos of the pamphlet warfare which during 1852 and 1853 was waged against the revival and the revivers of conventual life in the English Church. As in 1849, the object of attack was the Lady Superior of Devonport and Plymouth and her Society. It was not until the publication in November 1852 of the letters of the former Sister Charlotte White to a rejected Novice or "Child" of the Devonport Sisterhood, Miss Diana Campbell, that Sister Clara's abduction and rescue became known outside the narrow circle of those concerned. Miss White's references to the Regent's Park Community and the influence of Dr Pusey over its Sisters were as unfavourable as they were unjust. They implied the prevalence in Park Village West of the "abuses" alleged to exist at Devonport in the "anti-Sellon" tracts of the Reverend Messrs. Spurrell, Colles, and Cookesley, in the anti-Roman philippics of the Reverend Hobart Seymour, and in the tract of Miss Campbell herself. Written after her submission to the Roman Catholic Church, Miss Campbell's tract supported Mr Spurrell's charges, which had been refuted in Mother Lydia's *Reply*, published earlier in the year.

Mr Spurrell's pamphlet, entitled, *Miss Sellon and the Sisters of Mercy: An Exposure ... Obtained through a "Sister" Recently Seceded*, was concerned solely with Miss Sellon and her "system". There is no mention by name of the London Sisterhood. Mr Colles' tract, *Sisters of Mercy, Sisters of Misery*, although concerned pri-marily with the subject of its sub-title, "Miss Sellon in the Family", makes incidental reference to the Sisterhood in Regent's Park. It was the Reverend W. G. Cookesley who, in his *Letter to His Grace the Archbishop of Dublin*, published at the end of 1852 and reissued in

---

[1] [Cusack] *Five Years*, pp. 45–6. Miss Cusack's is one of two accounts of this service. She states explicitly that incense was not used. In the other account, which was published in *St Mary Magdalene's Parish Magazine*, December 1904, the writer is no less explicit in stating that "this was the first occasion on which incense was used in St Mary Magdalene's. ... The procession was headed by a cross-bearer. ... He was followed by the thurifer swinging the censer and accompanied by a boat-bearer." Mr Norman Shaw, a veteran member of the congregation, in a letter to the late Reverend W. H. H. Jervois, sometime vicar, gave 1854 as the date of the first use of incense. (It is possible that Miss Cusack was describing a similar service held at an earlier date than 1854.)

1853, brought the older Sisterhood into the controversy by his allegation that Dr Pusey had fleeced Miss White of her fortune. Dr Pusey's published reply stated the true facts concerning Miss White's connection with the Sisterhood, particularly her relation to the Orphans' Home. Before the publication of the Pusey–Cookesley correspondence, Mother Lydia's father, Commander Sellon, issued a circumstantial *Contradiction* of the charges of Messrs. Spurrell, Colles, and Seymour, against his daughter. This was followed by a communication to the daily press of a true account of Sister Clara's experience along with that Sister's and her mother's denials of the allegations and insinuations of Miss White.

Dr Pusey's rebuttal of Mr Cookesley's charges was not published until September 1853. In the meantime the relations between Regent's Park and Devonport had been made closer by the co-operation, as in the epidemic of 1849, of members of the two Communities in nursing the victims of a lighter outbreak of cholera at Plymouth in the summer and autumn of 1853. Although the number of the cases was fewer than in 1849, the ministrations of the Sisters (as the Devonport Mother reported to Bishop Phillpotts in a letter dated 14 January 1854) were required until a few weeks before the date of writing.

In the same letter Mother Lydia gave the Bishop an account of the extension of the work of her Society "into different dioceses, as persons living in those dioceses were willing to bear the expenses of these institutions".[1] She added that she had "been asked to take charge of a large Sisterhood in London". That the latter was the Sisterhood in Osnaburgh Street there can be no doubt, although one finds it hard to justify the use of the word "large" to describe a convent of not more than seven Religious. Nor can it be doubted that the invitation to "take charge" came from Dr Pusey, who by 1853 had become convinced that Mother Emma's "inexperience and want of decision" rendered her "unfit for her office", and that hope for the

---

[1] In the summer of 1851, at the invitation of Dr Monk, the Bishop of Gloucester and Bristol, Mother Lydia had inaugurated a convalescent hospital in Bristol in connection with two mission-houses and a home for the Sisters, the latter apparently at Brislington. In the same year a house was taken at Alverstoke, Gosport, and fitted up as a convent for the Sisters of the Sacred Heart, with provision for the care of orphans from Plymouth, patients from Bristol, and others in need of fresh air. In her letter to Bishop Phillpotts the Mother mentions also a "small hospital . . . in London and an almshouse and middle school in Berkshire". The "small hospital in London" was the "Nursing Sisters Home" in Pimlico mentioned by Miss Mary Stanley in *Hospitals and Sisterhoods* (pp. 53 ff).

future growth or even survival of the older Community lay in its being brought under the rule of the Lady Superior of Devonport.

A step in the desired direction was taken in 1853, when Mother Emma, at the wish of Dr Pusey, made a vow of obedience to the Devonport Superior, as previously recorded. Full and formal accomplishment of Dr Pusey's aim was not, however, to be realized until some three years later. But the course of events unforeseen in January made possible, even imperative, in October a further advance towards the desired goal. In October 1854 came a call for nurses to tend the sick and wounded soldiers of the British armed forces in the Crimea. Mr Sidney Herbert, the Secretary of State for War, had made the appeal to which Miss Florence Nightingale responded by undertaking to organize a band of nurses. These nurses were to be recruited partly from the better class of professional nurses, partly from "ladies" and women of the upper middle class. Two Roman Catholic Communities, the Sisters of Mercy of Bermondsey and the Community of the Faithful Virgin in Norwood, offered the services of members of their Societies. In a letter to *The Guardian* of 18 October, Earl Nelson (nephew of the hero of Trafalgar and one of the Committee of Laymen sponsoring the Park Village Community) urged "the heads of the few Sisterhoods in existence at that time" in the Church of England,[1] "to spare two or more Sisters each for nursing in the Crimea". He named in particular "Miss Sellon's Society" and the Communities at Wantage and Regent's Park. Mother Lydia had anticipated Lord Nelson's appeal by going up to London during the previous week to discuss with Miss Nightingale the possibility of sending out a party of Anglican Sisters. Several interviews followed during which the details of such an arrangement were discussed. "After a long conversation [Mother Lydia] consented to send out her Sisters under Miss Nightingale's authority."

Dr Pusey's approval was no doubt obtained before negotiations with Miss Nightingale were undertaken. Nothing had been said to

---

[1] The Communities existing at that time were the Sisterhood of the Holy Cross, Regent's Park; the Devonport Society of Sisters of Mercy; the Sisterhood at Wantage, known later as the Community of St Mary the Virgin; the Society of the Holy and Undivided Trinity, Oxford; the Community of St John Baptist, Clewer; and the Sisterhoods of St Thomas the Martyr, Oxford, and St Michael and All Angels, Bussage. A beginning had been made by Miss Byron and Mr Upton Richards towards the establishment of the Sisterhood now known as the All Saints Sisters of the Poor; and there was a Community of Nursing Sisters at St John's House in Fitzroy Square, London.

the Sisters of her own Society or the Superior of the London Community until these negotiations were satisfactorily concluded. Sister Clara relates in her account of early days, that "Mother Lydia suddenly arrived on Friday, 20 October, at St Saviour's and announced that she was sending a little band of Sisters under Miss Nightingale to Scutari" to nurse the sick and wounded there; that she wished Mother Emma to take charge and to choose some of her own Sisterhood to go with them. The whole arrangement", Sister Clara added, "was very sudden. On the fourth day"—Monday, 23 October— "they were on their way".

ABROAD
1854–1855

At the time when Mother Emma was bidden to choose members of her Community to join the Sisters from Devonport in the expedition to Scutari, there was resident at St Saviour's as an aspirant to the Religious Life a young lady from Wales, of Scottish birth, Miss Harriet Erskine, a daughter of Sir David Erskine, late of Cambo in Fife, Scotland. Miss Erskine's mother, the heiress of a Welsh clergyman, was residing with her daughters in her native Wales when Harriet expressed the wish to join the Sisterhood in Regent's Park. Although Lady Erskine "greatly disliked and entirely disapproved of the [conventual] system . . . she allowed her daughter to go on a visit to St Saviour's". As Miss Erskine had already had experience in nursing in her grandfather's parish and was a "certificated nurse", she was one of the two chosen by Mother Emma from her own household to accompany her and the Devonport Sisters to the East. When Lady Erskine received a letter stating that Harriet was on the way to Scutari, "she was pleased . . . hoping that it would turn her daughter's thoughts more to the life of a nurse than that of a Sister". Friends of Lady Erskine and her daughters in North Wales expected that "the knowledge this young lady had of the Welsh language would render her aid invaluable among the wounded Welsh". Sister Etheldreda was the other Sister of the Holy Cross chosen by Mother Emma to accompany her.

From the Sisters of the Devonport Society Mother Lydia chose five, of whom one, Sister Sarah Anne Terrot, was sometimes reckoned

—as by Miss Cusack—as one of the Regent's Park Sisters sent to Scutari. She was working in the Orphans' Home in Plymouth, when on Friday, 20 October, she received a peremptory summons to come at once to Osnaburgh Street, in company with Sister Amelia Warren and Sister Bertha Turnbull. Taking the mail train at 5 p.m., these Sisters were joined at Totnes by a Probationer for the rank of Lay Sister, Margaret Goodman, who had been summoned by telegram from the Society's Rest House at Asherne on the South Devonshire coast, and at Bristol by a Junior Sister of the Devonport Society, "Child" Clara Sharpe, who had been nursing in the Society's hospital in Bristol. None of the party knew why they had been summoned to London.

Arriving at 4 a.m. on Saturday morning, 21 October, the Sisters drove at once to St Saviour's. "There Sisters Catherine, Elizabeth, and Clara received them affectionately", but "did not enlighten them" as to the reason for their summons. Shortly after their arrival the Sisters were sent in turn to see Mother Lydia. They found her looking "ill and exhausted, scarcely able to speak. She said shortly, and with effort, 'Our soldiers in the East want nurses—some are going—I wish to send eight. Are you willing to be one?' " She explained to each Sister that "the work was one of peculiar danger, and that she would not be surprised if [a Sister] declined going". None declined. Rather were they all, like Sister Sarah Anne, "thankful and happy". Their answer, like hers, was a glad "Yes". Not in bed until 5 a.m., the Sisters were up at 7 o'clock and by 9 o'clock they were at Mr Sidney Herbert's house in Belgrave Square, waiting to receive their "papers of agreement" and Mr Herbert's instructions to the assembled nurses.

In addition to Sister Sarah Anne Terrot, Mother Lydia had chosen for the Devonport contingent of Sisters four others who had already shown aptitude for nursing: Sister Elizabeth Wheeler, who with Sister Sarah Anne had tended the victims of cholera at Plymouth in 1849 and 1853, and three who had done valiant service in the latter year: Sister Bertha Turnbull, Child[1] Clara Sharpe and the Lay Novice Margaret Goodman.

---

[1] The designation "Child" was conferred on members of the Society who had passed a term of noviceship determined by the Superior, but were not deemed ready to be "received as Sisters" by Profession of Life Vows. The status of a "Child" in the Devonport Society corresponded to that of a Junior Professed member of a modern Roman

It was while the Sisters were waiting at a neighbouring house in Belgrave Square to be summoned to Mr Herbert's that they first saw Miss Nightingale. Sister Sarah Anne "from the first felt an impulse to love, trust, and respect her. Her appearance and manner impressed her with a sense of goodness and wisdom, of high mental powers, highly cultivated and devoted to the highest ends". The assembled party of volunteers which met at Mr Herbert's house was composed of eighteen Sisters of Mercy—eight Anglican and ten Roman Catholic; six "nursing Sisters" from St John's Home in Fitzroy Square; three "lady nurses" selected by Lady Maria Forrester from groups less ecclesiastically suspect than the foregoing; and eleven professional nurses, carefully chosen from the large number—mostly of the "school of Sairey Gamp"—who applied for appointment.

"Mr Sidney Herbert, in his address, gave the two classes of nurses ... their respective cautions." To the secular nurses he "spoke of modesty and propriety"; to all of "enduring hardness". "To the Nuns and Sisters he said, 'Forbear teaching, and keep to the objects for which alone Government sends you out: the administering to the bodily wants, and soothing the minds, of the sick'. ... Both the Nuns and the ... Sisters were called upon to give their word that they would attempt no conversions." As they left Mr Herbert's house a lady of the Committee gave each of the Anglican Sisters "an immense railway rug, which proved a most acceptable gift", doing good service later as mattress, blanket, shawl, carpet, and screen.

After their return to Osnaburgh Street the Sisters "spent the rest of Saturday in preparatory needle-work". On Sunday morning they received Holy Communion together in St Mary Magdalene's Church. On that same evening at the service in the Oratory of St Saviour's at which Harriet Erskine and Margaret Goodman "received the habiliments of a Sister", Mother Emma was formally instituted Superior of the nursing party with the title of "Mother Eldress".[1]

Catholic or Anglican Community. The title "Child", like that of "Eldress" (see below), ceased to be used after the revision of the Statutes subsequent to the death of Mother Lydia.

[1] The title "Eldress", employed as a designation of certain members of the Devonport Society in its early days, was conferred in 1854 on those Sisters who had joined the Foundress in 1848 and 1849 in establishing the Society. Two of these senior Sisters were members of the Devonport contingent of nurses: Sister Sarah Anne Terrot and Sister Elizabeth Wheeler. The title "Mother Eldress" was borne by Sister Catherine

The Sisters of the Devonport Society who were to leave for the East on the morrow

took down from her mouth the following directions of their Superior:

"On quitting the house to mix with others, I warn you that your safety consists in adhesion (in spirit at least) to your Rule.

"In case of conscience apply to the Superior, and with her decision remain satisfied, as though you had committed it to myself.

"On the journey throughout observe silence among yourselves; and if persons speak to you, reply shortly, but courteously. Do not converse with anyone except Miss Nightingale, and not with her during your silence time.

"Be careful of the directions of the medical man, but never converse with him.

"Speak soothingly to the patients, but do not talk unnecessarily. Be reserved and courteous in manner.

"Be extremely neat and clean in person, that the Religious garb may be recommended by your manner of wearing it.

"In moments of excitement exercise extreme self-control. When you feel excited make an act of recollection of our Lord.

"Do not fast, and take all the care you can of your health; but do not let a day pass without an act of self-mortification.

"When you are attending to the wounds of the soldiers, try to think of the Wounds of our Lord. Keep calm as before the foot of His Cross, and remember that you are doing all things in Him. You will be greatly watched, and remember that on me will fall the consequence of little indiscretions on your part."

On Monday morning, 23 October, "about 6 a.m. the Sisters left St Saviour's for London Bridge Station, where they met again their sister nurses, about thirty in number, and five Nuns from the Convent of the Faithful Virgin (Norwood), [the latter] not in any conventual costume, but in simple black dresses. Mr and Mrs Bracebridge, friends of Mr and Mrs Herbert and Miss Nightingale, had preceded them to Paris" in company with Miss Nightingale. After a hurried breakfast in Folkestone the party went on board the Boulogne packet, amid the cheers of the crowds on the pier. The rough crossing

---

Chambers as Assistant Superior to Mother Lydia and by Mother Emma as the Mother's representative as head of the nursing party. The title was later defined in the Statutes of the Society as equivalent to "Prioress". The senior of the Eldresses in years, Sister Amelia Warren, bore the title of "Deane".

of the Channel proved too much for all but Mother Emma and Eldress Sarah Anne Terrot. But it was soon over. As the Sisters and nurses walked from the docks to the hotel, "the poor, merry-hearted porter women . . . insisted on carrying their luggage without payment".

Miss Nightingale had been accompanied to Paris by five Roman Catholic Sisters of Mercy from Bermondsey, whose Superior, Mother Clare, and another, Sister Mary Gonzaga, became two of Miss Nightingale's most trusted helpers and best beloved friends. On orders from Mr Herbert, Miss Nightingale and her companions were waiting in Paris for the second contingent before proceeding to Marseilles. After a railway journey to Lyons and a leisurely sail down the Rhône to Valence, the party reached Marseilles by train on Thursday, 26 October. The Anglican Sisters spent the time in their hotel, saying their Offices, working in silence at needle-work, and awaiting the call for meals as "being the chief event of the day and breaking the monotony". The Eldress Elizabeth and Sister Etheldreda, who were sent out to do some necessary shopping under the escort of the local British Chaplain, were impressed by the reverence paid to the Religious habit in a Catholic country, even by children. In fact, everywhere the Sisters and nurses met with kindly treatment: restaurateurs and hotel-keepers refused remuneration for food and lodging; porters and policemen were anxious to shake hands and display their knowledge of English.

On Friday, 27 October, Miss Nightingale and her party put out to sea in the mail packet, *Vectis*. The ship, "being intended for the transit of mail from Marseilles to Malta . . . was built entirely with a view to speed. . . . The beds of the crew, even in tolerable weather, were constantly saturated with spray". The Sisters and nurses travelled "steerage"; Miss Nightingale and the Bracebridges, "cabinclass". The quarters assigned to the Sisters were extremely crude. The fore-cabin of the hold was "divided into little recesses, each containing four berths like little shelves". The Anglican Sisters "were given the innermost recesses near the fore part of the boat, which were of course, the most confined and farthest from fresh air. . . . The [Roman Catholic] Nuns had a little division to themselves at the foot of the cabin stairs. The [secular] nurses lay in between". The Nuns, "who were best off for air, . . . paid for this advantage by having a double allowance of water, which the boat constantly shipped and which washed over the deck and down the cabin stairs".

H

The details of the voyage to Scutari—its dangers from storm and tempest, its discomforts from sea-sickness, vermin, and poor ventilation, its humorous as well as its distressing incidents, as related by the Eldress Sarah Anne and the Lay Novice Margaret Goodman in their respective *Reminiscences of Scutari Hospitals* and *Experiences of an English Sister of Mercy*, are related in a continuous narrative in *Priscilla Lydia Sellon*. In the present history of the Park Village Community only those happenings and experiences are recorded which concern the members of that Community or have relation to the progress of its history. During the rough passage aboard the *Vectis* and the first weeks spent in the Barracks Hospital at Scutari the relations between the Regent's Park and Devonport Sisters was so close that the story of one group is the story of the other. In the thought and words of Miss Nightingale and of other personnel of the hospital there was no distinction between Regent's Park and Devonport. The Sisters were all known as "Sellonites" or simply "Sellons".

The voyage from Marseilles to Malta was no rougher than might be expected on board such a craft as the *Vectis*. Two of the party who from experience knew themselves to be poor sailors, took to their beds as soon as possible after boarding the ship at Marseilles: Miss Nightingale in the comparative comfort of her state-room above stairs, Sister Bertha down below in "the close little box like a coffin, narrow and devoid of air, but full of crawling creatures", where she passed the rest of the voyage, employed during the brief intervals of freedom from sea-sickness in the massacre of the cockroaches and other vermin which infested the hold. Sister Etheldreda, whose health had been seriously impaired by the attack of small-pox of 1848, suffered less from sea-sickness than "from exhaustion and want of air". For relief she "had recourse to *eau de cologne*". She told the Eldress Sarah Anne that she "saved her life by drinking it". Her constant call for "Air! Air!" greatly puzzled one of the nurses, who remarked to Eldress Sarah Anne: "She is always calling for 'Air'. What does the lady mean? What does she want? Who is 'Air'?"—a question which suggested to Eldress Sarah Anne that the questioner was "as nobly ignorant of air and its functions as Lord Nelson was, when a child, of fear".

On the third day at sea, Monday, 30 October, early in the morning the *Vectis* made a stop at Valetta in the Island of Malta. All the party, except Sister Bertha and a few secular nurses, were taken ashore in little boats under the efficient escort of Mr Bracebridge. After a breathless tour of the city which included a visit to the Church of the Knights of St John of Malta, the Sisters were glad to return to their ship. That night a terrific storm arose which nearly sank the *Vectis* and terrified the passengers, especially the secular nurses. The Sisters, Roman and Anglican, who were not too sick or too exhausted to notice even the rolling and pitching of the ship, bore themselves with calm and resignation. Their less disciplined companions were filled with panic, screaming and moaning, praying for "Mercy, this once— only this once!" In this crisis Mother Emma exhibited the timidity and lack of assurance which had at length convinced Dr Pusey that she was "unfit for her office". When the terror and confusion were at the highest pitch, the Eldress Sarah Anne, having tried in vain to calm the screaming, scrambling nurses, "begged [Mother Emma] to use her efforts to soothe and quiet them; but she said very composedly, 'I have no authority. I cannot interfere' ".

There was, alas! worse to come. After the comparative calm of All Saints' Eve (31 October), All Saints' Day itself was ushered in shortly after midnight by "a fearful crash", followed by a pause more fearful than the crash. Most of the nurses and some of the Sisters were too exhausted to move. A few struggled to their feet; some "only sat up and looking around with a weary, bewildered gaze, sank back on the wet floor. . . . There was another pause: the ship seemed [to be] settling. . . . At length the watch-bell rang and a voice sang out, 'All's well'." A kind hearted officer soon came down to reassure "the poor things" with the announcement: "The worst is, I hope, over." Though the danger had been "evidently more real than on the former night . . . when the nurses were so excited . . . they seemed too sick . . . to care for danger".

At daybreak of All Saints' the Captain "kindly sent down some strong hot coffee". In the afternoon, when at the ship's-surgeon's orders the sick, "of whom the Sisters were the worst", were brought from the close sea-drenched cabin to the stern, "the brave Sister Bertha preferred to be alone in her little den, [where she had] lain day by day . . . without one murmur, but with the utmost resignation . . . cheerful and content with a basin beside her, and without outward amusement" save the slaughter of cockroaches. When Sister Etheldreda and Child Clara Sharpe "were carried in—miserable beings!" the Eldress Sarah Anne "could not help crying. . . . Sister Etheldreda was gasping, her face ashy white". She was put to bed on a table, "where she remained until the party reached Scutari".

During the course of All Souls' Day (2 November) a wave breaking over the bow washed overboard the steward's cabin, from which the steward was barely rescued before the cabin went over the side. That evening news was brought to the Sisters that the storm was abating.

10

"The Angel Band"
1854—1856

The Sisters found their quarters in the stern more comfortable than the cabin, and as the sea was comparatively calm, they spent a quiet night. The next morning (3 November) they found Miss Nightingale on deck looking very worn. The ship was nearing the entrance of the Dardanelles. At nightfall they entered the Sea of Marmora, where they drifted all night. "The next morning (4 November)... the Sisters found themselves lying, as it were, in the arms of the Queen of the East ... the great imperial Constantinople." In the course of the morning boats from Constantinople brought officials, attachés, and clergymen, and two French Sisters of Charity from Pera, to welcome Miss Nightingale. In the afternoon the *Vectis* began to move forward, "the clouds cleared, and the sun came out, the colour of sea and land exquisite".

But it was to "the ugliest object visible" that the Sisters gazed "with longing eyes"—"a great white building opposite Constantinople which they were told was the Scutari Barracks, where lay their sick and wounded countrymen". Miss Nightingale and the Bermondsey Sisters of Mercy left the *Vectis* early in the morning, accompanied by the secular nurses. The eight Anglican Sisters were kept waiting on board—as they afterwards learned—until the body of a Russian General, who had died at Scutari as a prisoner of war, could be removed from the apartment assigned to the Sisters in the Barracks. It was, therefore, late evening when "they crossed the straits in *caïques*, four of them in each". The Sisters were beginning to feel refreshed and inspirited by the novel experience of being rowed through the water in these "luxurious conveyances", as they lay on cushions in the bottom and "the picturesque rowers sat above them on benches". But their spirits fell when they reached the landing

pier at Scutari and beheld the wretched appearance of the few soldiers and even more miserable looking women who stood about the
dilapidated wharf awaiting their arrival. The carcase of a large grey
horse, washed almost within the reach of a pack of hungry dogs, only
to be carried away by the ebb of the tide, completed the gaunt deso-
lation of the scene and blotted out the impression of the beautiful
landscape.

The Sisters climbed out of their *caïques* on to the pier and struggled
up the steep hill to the hospital. The Sisters' living quarters were
situated in one of the four towers which stood at the angles of the
building. Here Miss Nightingale, the Bracebridges, and the Roman
Catholic Sisters were also housed. In contemporary plans and drawings this tower is designated "The Sisters' Tower". The discomforts
of the Anglican Sisters and their ministrations to the sick and wounded, who suffered more than discomforts in the wards, are graph-
ically recorded in the letters written by the Sisters and in the published
Experiences of Miss Goodman and the privately printed *Reminiscences* of Miss Terrot.[1]

The two Eldresses, Elizabeth and Sarah Anne, were assigned to the
cholera wards of the Barracks Hospital, which were filled, not with
cholera patients, but with men recently arrived from the battlefield
of Balaclava, suffering from "exposure to damp and cold, fatigue,
and insufficient food". Mother Eldress Emma and Sister Etheldreda
were unable to eat the rough, often scanty, fare at first provided. The
Mother Eldress, however, found a sustaining diet in the figs, grapes,
and oranges, which were plentiful and cheap, and in "the pure and
pleasant drink . . . much in use in the hospital"—rice-water. She
was, in consequence, able to carry on the work assigned to her, with
the capable assistance of the Novice Harriet Erskine. The Devonport
Lay-Probationer, Margaret Goodman, from her first assignment in
the General Hospital, which was at some distance from the Barracks,
was the companion or "shadow" of the capable Scottish Sister Bertha
Turnbull. Sister Etheldreda's inability to eat the coarse food or to

[1] The Crimean Letters of the Devonport Sisters have been preserved in the archives
of Ascot Priory. Extracts were published in *Vigilate*, the "occasional paper" of the
Ascot Community, during 1930 and 1931. Several interesting details about the Regent's
Park Sisters related by Mrs Cecil Woodham Smith in her biography of *Florence Nightingale*, which were not known when *Priscilla Lydia Sellon* was written, have been incorporated in the present history, along with a few data derived from letters of Miss
Nightingale and Miss Langston.

receive sufficient nourishment from the fruit diet of the Mother Eldress so greatly aggravated the weakness resulting from her illness on board the *Vectis* that she was never well enough to be assigned duty in the wards. Early in December she was sent home. Miss Goodman's dislike of conventual observances led her to attribute Sister Etheldreda's rejection to her alleged insistence on observing even in the hospital the rule of the Sisterhood of the Holy Cross that the Sisters walk with bowed head and downcast eyes in a public place. Miss Terrot's and other contemporary statements prove that at least the primary cause of her "being sent home without having laboured in the wards for one hour" was the Sister's ill health.

The Eldress Elizabeth, in her distress at the lack of proper and sufficient food for her patients, to say nothing of the Sisters and other nurses, had written and dispatched two letters without Miss Nightingale's knowledge or authorization—one to relatives of her sister's husband in London, the other to her Superior—asking, in the first instance, for food and other comforts for the soldiers; in the latter, for "a box of captain's biscuits and a good English cheese" for the Sisters. The ship which brought the box containing these and other "good things" from Plymouth was wrecked on November 14 by a hurricane which rocked the Sisters' Tower at the Barracks and blew in some of the windows. The response to the Eldress' appeal for comforts for the soldiers was less immediate. The publication of her letter in *The Times* of 8 December and later in *The Guardian* and *The Illustrated London News* not only effected the dispatch to Scutari of the provisions asked for, but also raised an outcry of indignation in official circles against the inferred negligence on the part of Government[1] and an equally indignant demand on the part of the military officials in the East that the writer of the letter be identified, reprimanded, convicted of falsehood, and dismissed from service. All which measures were promptly taken, without giving the "culprit" a fair hearing. In the sentence passed by the "court martial" Miss Nightingale concurred. The name of Elizabeth Wheeler was stricken from the Register of Nurses, her nurses' badge removed, and she herself ordered home on the next vessel sailing from Constantinople.

---

[1] Eldress Elizabeth was at pains in her letter to exonerate the Government from blame for the conditions described. But these passages were overlooked by those who were eager for an excuse to attack the Government and to discredit Miss Nightingale and her staff. The Eldress' letter is quoted in *Priscilla Lydia Sellon*.

Sentence was passed on 23 December. The next day, Christmas Eve, Miss Nightingale gave notice that Eldress Elizabeth must be ready to leave for England that evening on board the *Candia*. The Eldress Sarah Anne was given permission to accompany her to the landing pier beneath the hospital, to bid farewell to her beloved companion and to the other Devonport Sister, Child Clara, who had a few days earlier been "released from service" as being "disqualified for nursing". Returning to England in the same ship were the five "angels without hands", as Miss Nightingale called the white Nuns of the Company of the Faithful Virgin from Norwood, who had likewise been found to be "disqualified for nursing".

Christmas 1854 was a sad time for the Sisters who remained in the East. The sadness was mitigated by the comfort of Christmas Communion and by the pathetic effort of the men in the wards to provide a surprise treat for the Sisters in the shape of "Christmas puddings" concocted of eggs, fat, and flour begged from the diet kitchen through the confidential negotiations of Novice Margaret Goodman—the said puddings being secreted under the pillows of the patients until they could be smuggled to the kitchen for boiling.

Christmastide at home was saddened for the Sisters of the Holy Cross by the death, two days after Christmas "in great peace" of Sister Jane Ellacombe, at her father's rectory at Clyst St George, Devon. Not long after Mother Lydia took up residence at St Saviour's, Sister Jane was permitted to go for a visit to her father, whom she had not seen for nine years. The cause of her death is stated in the certificate of the same to have been "phthisis pulmonaris", which had apparently made so little headway that her sister, writing to Canon Liddon many years later, supposed that Sister Jane "died without any particular disease, worn out", she suggested, by "the bodily austerities of nine years". The official record indicates that her father was with her when she died. Dr Pusey had written to Mr Keble in the previous October that he was "going to see Sister Jane, who was dying, near Exeter" (at Clyst St George), "and to see the Devonport Mother, who" Dr Pusey was sure Mr Keble would be "sorry to know", "was required to have more decided rest". In a letter written to Sister Clara on the day after Sister Jane's death, Dr Pusey's language implies that he too had been present at her deathbed: "Will you tell those who knew and loved Sister Jane that she fell asleep in our Lord very peacefully yesterday? She had been waiting her end in much stillness, but longing to be dissolved and be with our Lord." Her one-time spiritual guide, John Henry Newman, to whose teaching she owed her first aspiration to the dedicated virgin state, wrote from the Oratory in Birmingham to thank Mr Ellacombe for letting him know of his daughter's death and to offer him consolation in the thought that she had given her life as "a sacrifice to her strong religious feelings". Mr Ellacombe survived his daughter some thirty years, never ceasing to sorrow for his bereavement, but "regarding with unabated affection and respect the preacher to whose exaggerated tone, as he felt, he owed what had befallen him". Sister Jane's body lies in the churchyard of her father's former parish of Bitton in Gloucestershire, her birthplace.

It was during 1854 that Miss Lucy Watkins, who had been "pledged to the Sisterhood" for several years but was hindered by a previous engagement from coming to St Saviour's, having at length fulfilled her engagement, began her Probation in the Sisterhood of the Holy Cross. Miss Watkins was one of the eight daughters of William Watkins, Esq., late of Badby House, Northants. In 1851 she and four of her sisters moved to Wantage in Berkshire, where the new vicar, the Reverend William John Butler, was in pressing need of competent school-mistresses. Miss Watkins, with one of her sisters, volunteered for service with the understanding that as soon as a suitable mistress could be found to take her place she would be free to go to St Saviour's. Her coming to the Sisterhood was timely. The departure of the Superior and two of the Sisters for the East had reduced the number of Sisters of the Holy Cross resident at St Saviour's to four, or, at most, five Sisters and two Probationers.[1] Sister Jane's death reduced the number further. Mother Lydia was able to bring Sisters from Plymouth to Regent's Park when she came to assume temporary charge of St Saviour's. The two Probationers were transferred to houses of the Devonport Society. The effect of these interchanges was to unite the two Communities under the Devonport Mother on

[1] One of the Sisters was Margaret Hooper, later of Clewer. It is not known whether Sister Caroline Paul, who was in residence at No. 17 Park Village West, as a "Sister of Mercy" in 1851, was still in the Community in 1855. Sister Clara had been formally received into the Devonport Society as a "Child" of the Second Order. Sister Etheldreda had returned from the East before the end of 1854. She and Sister Jane were the two Sisters of the Holy Cross still in England before Sister Jane's death in December, Sister Caroline Paul being a possible third. The two Probationers were Miss Cusack and Miss Watkins.

a temporary basis until the complete union, desired by Dr Pusey, could be permanently effected.

Miss Cusack alleged that Mother Lydia had "so arranged matters" —with whom arranged she does not state—that Sister Etheldreda, Sister Sarah Anne, whom Miss Cusack always reckoned as a member of the Regent's Park Community, and Mother Emma "should not meet" after their arrival at Scutari, "or if they did meet, they should have no opportunity of conversing together". Whether Mother Lydia actually tried to make such a preposterous "arrangement" or not, it is certain that no such fantastic procedure was followed in Miss Nightingale's assignment of these Sisters to duty. For the first few days, before assignments could be made, and even afterwards, until Eldress Sarah Anne, Sister Bertha, and Novice Margaret were sent to live as well as work in the General Hospital, the Regent's Park Sisters ate and slept and said their Offices in the same apartment in the "Sisters' Tower" at the Barracks Hospital. From the first day of actual service in the wards, Novice Harriet Erskine, the Probationer from Regent's Park, worked with the Regent's Park Superior, Mother Emma. When in January 1855 Lord Raglan "authorized the hospital authorities to ask for eight" nurses to be sent to the Crimea, Miss Nightingale appointed Mother Emma superintendent of the party. Mother Emma had never been happy in working "under" Miss Nightingale. Like the Eldress Elizabeth, she found it hard to grasp the essential point at issue, that in a military hospital absolute conformity to military rules must be observed. Furthermore, Mother Emma was constitutionally and temperamentally "unfitted to govern", being unable to command the necessary deference to her authority of the Devonport Sisters. It was for these reasons, Miss Nightingale wrote to Mother Lydia, that the London Mother was sent to the Crimea. In March, at Mother Emma's request, Sister Harriet Erskine was sent to assist her Superior.

Miss Nightingale had been reluctant to send nurses to the Crimea, which she thought was "no place for women just then". The sanitary conditions were notoriously bad, the military authorities were known to be hostile to Miss Nightingale, and the conduct of the secular nurses already at Balaclava was scandalous. Some of the volunteers from Scutari had offered their services in the Crimea in order to escape from the rule of Miss Nightingale, who for various reasons had incurred their dislike.

By March the situation was beyond the control of the timid, vacillating Mother Eldress, who (to quote Miss Nightingale) "lost her head and her health", collapsed, and towards the end of April, as she was "thought to be dying of fever", she was placed on a stretcher and taken aboard a ship sailing for Constantinople. The Secretary of the British Embassy, Lord Napier, brother of the some-time Sister Georgiana, whose wife had known Miss Langston "in her worldly days", kindly offered to receive the Mother Eldress into his home. Novice Harriet and a secular nurse returning on sick-leave to Scutari accompanied her. During a storm in the Black Sea the dying Mother Eldress was "rolled out of bed". But "this rough treatment", instead of hastening her death, "seemed to bring a reaction. She began to rally, and though still very ill, arrived at Constantinople in a much less hopeless condition than that in which she had left the Crimea".

When the party arrived at the landing pier at Constantinople, there was no one to receive them and no conveyance available to take them to Lord Napier's residence. They remained tossing in an open boat moored to the pier until an officer, observing their plight, asked if he could in any way assist them. Novice Harriet said that she wished some conveyance to take them to Lord Napier's. The officer went away but soon returned with some soldiers who lifted the stretcher and mattress on which the Mother Eldress lay out of the boat and carried her to Lord Napier's, accompanied by "the zealous and trust-worthy" Novice Harriet.[1]

Meantime, another of Miss Nightingale's "poor Sellons", the "single-minded, most worthy" Eldress Sarah Anne, broke down under the strain of work in the pestilential air of the Barracks Hospital and, later, of the General Hospital and by the daily journey in all weathers to and from the latter. Her condition was not bettered by her stinting

---

[1] "Zealous and trustworthy" are the terms used to characterize both Miss Erskine and Miss Goodman in the memorandum, already cited, preserved at Ascot Priory, in which is recorded Miss Nightingale's estimate of the several members of the Regent's Park–Devonport contingent of nurses. The highest praise is given to Sister Bertha Turnbull of the Devonport Society, who is described as "excellent"—under-scored. The Eldress Sarah Anne is described as "single-minded, most worthy"; Mother Emma as "too old, no memory; fussy"; Sister Etheldreda, as "too delicate"; Child Clara had "awkward but gentle and good hands"—or was herself "awkward but gentle and [had] good hands". The characterization of the Eldress Elizabeth represents Miss Nightingale's estimate at the time when she was annoyed by the Eldress' *trop de zèle*, but would seem, in the light of the high esteem in which she was held by the Eldress Sarah Anne, to have been as unjust as it was frank.

herself of the none too generous nurses' rations, in order that "her men" might have a little butter—wretched as it was—or a sandwich. The fever from which she suffered was not contagious nor did it prove fatal, although her death was expected at any time during ten days or a fortnight. She came to be known among her companion nurses as "the lady who *would* not die". Her convalescence was slow, retarded by her dread of being "released from service" and invalided home, to face anew the "trial and perplexity" of increasing doubt as to her fitness for conventual life. She suffered less harm from the experience of an earthquake which one night shook the bed on which she lay "expecting to see the roof fall and [herself] swallowed up"— yet wholly unafraid. Soon after the earthquake she received orders to make ready for her return to England. Her packing was quickly done. Presents offered by her admirers (including a barrel of wine) were declined in accordance with the Rule of the Devonport Society. A few days before the date set for departure, the Eldress was permitted to go to Constantinople to visit Mother Emma, whom she found steadily improving.

II

On the Home Front
1855—1856

A letter among the Nightingale Papers in the British Museum[1] indicates that at the date of writing, 15 March 1855, Miss Nightingale expected within a few days to send Mother Emma and the Eldress Sarah Anne to England on the same boat, the screw steamer *Adelaide*. Neither, however, was strong enough to travel when the sailing date arrived. Eldress Sarah Anne sailed on the *Cange*, by way of Piraeus, where Miss Mary Stanley, under Miss Nightingale's merited displeasure, was expected to join the party from Scutari. Miss Stanley, however, had not arrived when Eldress Sarah Anne reached Piraeus. The Eldress took advantage of the stop to pay a hurried visit to Athens between the arrival and departure of the *Cange*. After a smooth voyage from Piraeus to Marseilles, more comfortable, if less exciting, than the rough passage some six months before in the hold of the *Vectis*, the Eldress under the escort of a physician who also was returning to England from the East,[2] took the night train at Marseilles for Boulogne; thence by packet to England. Arrived in London she bade her "kind escort" good-bye and proceeded by cab to Osnaburgh Street. She was soon sent to Bristol to work among the poor whom she loved.

Miss Terrot had been thrice a pioneer. She was one of the first to join the little company of women who in 1845 initiated the revival of the Religious Life in the Church of England. She was one of the Sisters who in 1849 and again in 1853, during the cholera epidemics of those years, defied convention and prejudice to prove that the service of nursing need not be confined to "the likes of Sairey Gamp",

---

[1] General Correspondence and Papers during the Crimean War, 1854–6, No. 52.
[2] This was Dr Smyth, whose regular attendance at Holy Communion had been noted by the Sisters.

and in so doing opened the way for the achievements of Florence Nightingale.[1] She was one of the most useful and trusted members of the first group of "lady nurses" to serve in British Military Hospitals.

At an early stage of her life as a Sister of the Holy Cross at No. 17 Park Village West, Miss Terrot manifested a disregard for the details of monastic observance which caused anxiety to Dr Pusey. He was, however, reassured by Mr Dodsworth, who "did not think Sister Sarah was more to blame than the rest". When Miss Sellon visited the Community in Regent's Park in 1848, she confessed to Sister Sarah Anne that "the strictness of the Rule appalled her". When Sister Sarah Anne joined the household at Devonport in 1849, she found the life of the Sisters there domestic rather than monastic. A few simple rules were tentatively adopted until a more formal and detailed system could be developed in the light of experience and the study of established conventual Rules and observances.[2] Miss Terrot later described the household at Devonport in 1849 as "the happiest, busiest, least constrained, and most united of any she was ever in; not unlike", she alleged, "but the very opposite of all it was when she left [the Society] in 1855". She admitted that she "had ever refused to be subjected to" the rules imposed at Devonport during her absence in the East, as she had struggled for some three years against the minutiae of the Park Village Rule. The expedition to Scutari had afforded temporary respite from "the trial and anxiety" caused by the gradual, "almost

[1] The significance of the early ventures of Mother Lydia and her Sisters in the field of nursing as a "blazing of the trail" in preparation for Miss Nightingale's accomplishment, was recognized by a correspondent of *The Guardian* (3 October 1855), who in drawing attention to "the neglect which, during the outburst of enthusiasm for Miss Nightingale, her fore-runner, Miss Sellon, had experienced", added that "it was not too much to say that if it had not been for Miss Sellon and her Sisterhood, the public never would have found toleration for Miss Nightingale and her band of nurses". If Miss Sellon "had not met the public prejudice against Sisterhoods, fought a desperate battle against it . . . preparing the country to accept a somewhat lower system, there would have been such an outcry against Miss Nightingale's organized band of nurses as must have been injurious to its welfare. As it was", the writer concluded, "there was outcry enough." In 1878, two years after the death of Mother Lydia, Archdeacon Ffoulkes, in presenting a resolution in the Lower House of the Convocation of Canterbury on the subject of Sisterhoods and Deaconesses, reminded his hearers that "the value of Sisterhoods had been brought before the eyes of the nation by the Crimean War" in such a way that the name of Miss Sellon "would be long remembered" with the name of Miss Nightingale, "as having taught the people [of Britain] the value of women's work". Alas! it has not been so remembered.

[2] For an analysis of the form and sources of the Rule of the Devonport Society, especially the Statutes, between 1848 and 1861, the reader is referred to *Priscilla Lydia Sellon.*

imperceptible" developments in the Devonport Society which five years later induced the Novice Margaret Goodman to return to her previous life in the world as a school-mistress.[1]

It was the enforcement of one of the allegedly new rules which caused Miss Terrot to resolve her doubts and perplexities by withdrawing from the Devonport Society in the September of 1855— the rule that letters addressed to a Sister must pass through the hands of the Superior before delivery to the destined recipient. When a letter arrived from Edinburgh informing Eldress Sarah Anne of the serious illness of her mother, its delivery was delayed because of the absence of the Superior when it arrived. In consequence of her delay in receiving the letter, Eldress Sarah Anne did not reach Edinburgh until after her mother's death. "Deeply hurt . . . [she] felt herself justified in severing her connection with the Sisterhood", especially as she was not one of those who on being received as a Sister in the Park Village Community "had taken or renewed" the Vows of Religion. "The severance caused her intense pain"; but after the first shock of resentment was past, "it left no bitterness, and to the end of her life she spoke of [the Superior] . . . and of the Sisters with affectionate appreciation."[2] For a time Miss Terrot was associated with Miss

[1] Miss Goodman left the Society in 1859, having been refused admission to Profession after seven years of Probation. After three years of teaching in girls' schools in Cheltenham and Inverness repectively, she was recommended by Miss Nightingale for the position of Matron of the Birmingham General Hospital, which she held during the years 1863-4. In 1862 she published *Experiences of an English Sister of Mercy*, followed in 1863 by *Sisterhoods in the Church of England* (Second Edition, 1864), which Miss Nightingale, in a note at the end of the Appendix to the third edition of her *Notes on Hospitals and Nursing*, characterized as "two excessively foolish books by the same woman, calling herself an 'English Sister of Mercy' . . . in which the difficulty was, not to find what is false, but to find what is true" (quoted in the Reverend A. M. Allchin, *The Silent Rebellion*, p. 124). During the Franco-Prussian War Miss Goodman volunteered for nursing service at the Front. After this, nothing further is known of her.

[2] *The Scottish Standard Bearer* (September 1901), pp. 198–9: "The late Sarah Anne Terrot". Her sister, Miss Katherine Terrot, who for a brief time in 1844–5 thought of joining the proposed Community in Park Village West, after displaying "Roman tendencies", eventually became (in succession) a Methodist, a member of the Plymouth Brethren, and several other sects, returning at last to the Scottish Episcopal Church as a member of a very "Low Church" congregation in Edinburgh. The youngest of the Misses Terrot, Anna Jemima, joined the Devonport Society in the 1860s as a Sister of Charity of the Third Order, working among the poor in East London until her advanced age made necessary her retirement in 1906. In 1877 was published *Scenes from the Life of the First Benedictines*, "by Anna J. Terrot, English Sister of Charity", with a dedication to Dr Pusey. "The proceeds of this little work, if any, were to be devoted to the relief of the sick poor of Spitalfields and Bethnal Green." Sister Anna died at Cumbernauld, Scotland, 30 July 1916.

Nightingale at St Thomas' Hospital in London as a "supernumerary [who] supplemented the Matron's reports" in the Nightingale School of Nursing. Later she engaged in "ministries to the suffering in Edinburgh and several English parishes". The last ten years of her active life she spent as head of a small orphanage for girls at Culross in Fife. It was from there that she was summoned in 1897 to Balmoral Castle to be invested by Queen Victoria with the Royal Red Cross in tardy "acknowledgement of her services to the Queen's soldiers in 1854". Miss Terrot died on 10 July 1901, after two years of increasing helplessness, "without one murmuring word", like her one-time Sister in Religion, Jane Ellacombe, "longing to be dissolved and be with our Lord".

The steps toward union of the Sisterhood of the Holy Cross with the Society of Sisters of Mercy of Devonport and Plymouth were taken with deliberation, though at times falteringly. Sister Clara has left in her Reminiscences of the Park Village Community, which she wrote for the information of Canon Liddon,[1] a fuller account of these steps than has heretofore been available. They supply details concerning the Park Village Sisterhood between the end of 1854 and the final union of the two Communities in 1856, which give a more reliable picture of the situation and of the steps which led to the union than the account given by Miss Cusack in *Five Years in a Protestant Sisterhood* and *The Story of my Life*. They supplement with significant details the outlines given in memoranda preserved at Ascot Priory.

The suggestion that St John's House in Fitzroy Square and St Saviour's Home in Osnaburgh Street should afford accommodation and training for women ready to volunteer as nurses in the East, met with ready response. "St Saviour's . . . became a house for persons wishing to be trained as nurses for the war, and it was advisable for Mother Lydia to reside there." To reinforce the depleted numbers of the Community at St Saviour's, she "called up" Sisters from Plymouth. At first "each Society observed its own Rule. But this did not last long. In the Spring [of 1855] they again separated. . . .

[1] These reminiscences were used sparingly by Dr Liddon in his account of the Park Village Sisterhood in Volume III of his *Life of E. B. Pusey* (Chapter I). Their existence was forgotten for many years until they were discovered by Mr Allan W. Campbell in the library of Pusey House, Oxford, and by permission of the Principal of the House and the co-operation of Mr Robert Cover were made available for use in the present work.

One of the oldest of the Sisters of the Holy Cross [Sister Etheldreda] became Superior" of the Regent's Park Community, retaining that office "until the return of Mother Emma". Dr Pusey interpreted the action of the Regent's Park Sisters as "rebellion" against Mother Lydia, who, he claimed, "was turned out of St Saviour's by some rebels against their then Superior".

Her "expulsion" from St Saviour's afforded Mother Lydia more time for perfecting and carrying out her plans for mission work among the poor of East London. She "procured a house near Spitalfields",[1] which was opened by Dr Pusey with a solemn service and blessing.

---

[1] Both Dr Pusey and Mother Lydia were deeply concerned for the spiritual, moral, and material welfare of the inhabitants of this section of East London—both of them because of their respective ancestral connections through the Bouveries and the Sellons with the Huguenot forebears of a large percentage of the population of Spitalfields and Bethnal Green. Mother Lydia was particularly concerned for the wretched conditions of the dwelling accommodation of these folk, the criminal character of most of their neighbours, and the lack of spiritual and educational opportunities of the district. One particular section seemed to haunt her: the neighbourhood of Flower and Dean Street between Commercial Street and Brick Lane, which was at that time one of the worst rookeries in London. From the time when she established a temporary cholera hospital in a vacant warehouse in 1866 until her last years, she made repeated efforts to acquire property in the street with a double name and a dubious reputation, planning at one time to make her residence in the said Flower and Dean Street. Many of her letters to the second Lord Halifax (at that time the Hon. Charles Wood) written between 1866 and 1876 are concerned with her plans for this part of East London. The property in the street which she wished to "redeem" she never acquired. But many years later her vision of its "redemption" was realized, at least in its material aspect, by the erection of the Rothschild Flats and other substitutes for the disreputable and dilapidated hovels of Mother Lydia's day. A visitor to the neighbourhood in the present time finds it hard to believe that this was at one time—as late as the 1880s—one of the worst sections of East London. The most Mother Lydia was able to accomplish was to establish a small Mission House, with a Soup Kitchen and Dispensary attached, in the neighbourhood of Brick Lane. From these centres the Sisters of Charity of the Third Order of her Society ministered to the bodies and souls of some 1,600 families in twelve parishes in East London.

12

Union 1856

The following account of the union of the Regent's Park Sisterhood of the Holy Cross with the Devonport Society of Sisters of Mercy is based on documents found at Ascot Priory and Pusey House, Oxford, supplemented by data derived from Sister Clara's reminiscences. One of the Ascot documents is a memorandum in the handwriting of Sister Clara. Another memorandum, dated 21 November 1900, apparently embodies the reminiscences of Miss Mary Kebbel, whose association with the Regent's Park Sisterhood began as early as 1847. A third, more formal but briefer, document is a summary of significant data some of which are not included in the other memoranda. Outstanding in importance are letters of Mother Emma Langston, addressed to the Mother Eldress Catherine in 1854, and of Mother Lydia's successor, Sister Bertha Turnbull, giving information to Dr Liddon concerning the union of the two Communities.

When Mother Emma returned from the East it was expected by most of the Sisters of the Holy Cross that she would be reinstated at St Saviour's as Superior of their Community. In anticipation of this Sister Etheldreda resigned from the office of "head" to which she had been appointed when the Devonport Mother was "turned out" of St Saviour's. But when Mother Emma, after a brief stay in Bristol, came to London and saw the "deadened state" of affairs—"the finances unable to meet the expenses, the property mortgaged for £3,000"— she was confirmed in her long cherished desire, frequently expressed of late, to resign to Mother Lydia the office for which her frail health disqualified her. In letters written from Scutari to the Mother Eldress Catherine of the Devonport Society Mother Emma repeatedly expressed an earnest wish for the union of her Community with the younger Society and her desire to be herself entirely in subjection to the Devonport Mother. While admitting that he was "satisfied that the union of the two Sisterhoods would benefit that in

London", Dr Pusey insisted that the union was "solely at the London Mother's seeking" as something she had long wished for. "He had scrupulously refrained from using his influence" in favour of the union.

Mother Emma "begged Mother Lydia to take the superintendence and effect a union" of the two Communities. In 1883 there was in the safe at St Dunstan's, Plymouth, a copy of Mother Emma's address to the Sisters of the Holy Cross "explaining that if [the Devonport Mother] had not taken St Saviour's, it must have collapsed, it was so desperately in debt". Miss Cusack's allegation that Mother Emma was one of those of the older Community opposed to the union, although devoted to Dr Pusey and outwardly loyal to Mother Lydia, can be credited only on the impossible supposition that Mother Emma's frequent expressions of loving devotion to Mother Lydia and of her strong and long-standing desire for the union of the two Communities were insincere.

Equally unworthy of credit, in the face of contemporary documentary evidence, are Miss Cusack's repeated statements that Mother Lydia contrived the union of the two Sisterhoods in order to satisfy her ambition. Not only do Mother Emma's letters, already cited, contradict Miss Cusack's allegations, but in 1883 Mother Lydia's successor, Mother Bertha Turnbull, assured Dr Liddon that from what the Devonport Mother told her at the time when the union of the Communities was effected, she did not think that when, in deference to the wishes of Dr Pusey and Mother Emma, she undertook to weld the two Communities into one, she "liked doing it at all", and that the older Devonport Sisters, including herself, "could not bear" the changes brought about by the union through the introduction of "rules and views which the Devonport Sisters did not like". It was Dr Pusey, Mother Bertha averred, who persuaded Mother Lydia to take charge of St Saviour's again and of the Sisters who remained in the London Community. Mother Lydia did not, however, give up the work among the poor weavers of East London, which she had fought so valiantly to maintain in the face of episcopal hostility. Mother Emma was placed in charge of the Mission House and Soup Kitchen in Spitalfields. Mother Lydia sent to help her the sometime Probationer of the older Community, Margaret Anna Cusack, who after a brief withdrawal had returned to be received into the Devonport Society as a "Visitor on Probation".

The contrast between the gentle, timid rule of Mother Emma and the vigorous administration of Mother Lydia was unwelcome to some of the Sisters of the older Community and was no doubt a contributing cause of rebellion against her rule. The Devonport Mother was suspected of trying to keep the Sisters of the Holy Cross from association with one another not only in the East but in England as well. She was even accused by Miss Cusack of interfering with the free access of the Sisters to Dr Pusey, both in the confessional and in their non-sacramental relations with him as their spiritual director.[1] The members of the Committee of Laymen responsible for the financial support of the older Sisterhood are reported to have been unfavourable to the absorption of that Community by the Devonport Society. Sister Etheldreda and Novice Margaret Anna Cusack were among those who were opposed to the union. Sister Clara, who had been the largest contributor to the establishment of St Saviour's through her purchase of the ground-lease, which was still held in trust in her name, was one of those whose hearts "one by one were drawn to Devonport" as early as 1851. She had, in fact, been received as a Child of that Society in 1854, probably at the time when Mother Lydia first assumed control at St Saviour's. It was in that year that Novice Margaret Anna was transferred from her probationership in the Regent's Park Community to the novitiate of the Devonport Society and sent to the house of the Nuns of the Sacred Heart in Bristol. Miss Cusack developed an implacable hatred of Mother Lydia. Nevertheless, on returning from a visit to an ageing aunt, she placed herself under Mother Lydia's rule in the status of a visitor on probation, as previously noted. As assistant to Mother Emma in the Mission House in Spitalfields she worked happily among the weavers of the district. In addition to her ministrations to the poor, Mother Emma had been entrusted with the care of a psychopathic patient, a young girl whose family was in India. Miss Langston's calmness gave her a power over the mentally deranged which in 1853 she had exercised with singular and dramatic effect over a mad-woman in the Sisters' care at Asherne, where they had the use as a rest-house of a fishing and hunting lodge on a cliff overhanging Start Bay. Deter-

---

[1] Miss Cusack's charges (*Five Years*, pp. 97–8, and *The Story of My Life*, pp. 71–2) are too preposterous to be credited by anyone acquainted with the character of Dr Pusey. They are as lacking in truth as her charge as to Mother Lydia's alleged attempt to keep the Sisters of the Holy Cross apart from one another at Scutari.

mined to "go to glory" by leaping from the cliff, the patient success-
fully resisted every physical effort to restrain her, but was subdued by
Mother Emma's steady eye and calm presence of mind. Miss Cusack
continued to work among the poor of Spitalfields and Bethnal Green
until in the summer of 1858 her restless disposition led her into the
Roman Catholic Church.[1]

Two years before Miss Cusack's defection Mother Emma left the
Devonport Society and the Church of England to be received into
the Roman Catholic Church—some two weeks before the final
formalities of the union of the two Communities to which she had
belonged. In 1857 she applied to Miss Nightingale for her share in
the "Sultan's Gift" or bonus, granted to the nurses who had served
in the East. Being too late in her application, she received a personal
gift from Miss Nightingale for use among the poor. Miss Langston's
further history is unknown beyond the fact that she made a gift of all
her jewellery to Brompton Oratory for the purchase of a ciborium.
There can be little doubt, however, that Miss Langston was "the
lady", described by Miss Goodman as "an apostate from our Faith,
for some years the Superior of an Anglican Sisterhood", who in
seeking to continue her life in Religion as a Roman Catholic, "had
tried five convents and had been rejected in every instance by the

---

[1] In 1859, after an unsatisfactory experience as an aspirant to the life of a Dominican
under Mother Margaret Hallanan at Stone, Miss Cusack returned to her native Ireland
to enter the Novitiate of the Irish Poor Clares at Newry. After Profession she was transferred to Kenmare, where she distinguished herself by her ability to raise funds for
famine relief in 1879, winning for herself fame and popular esteem as "The Nun of
Kenmare". During her career as a Roman Catholic Religious she produced an un-
believably large number of books of Irish history and biography, pious fiction, devotional books, and collections of rhymes and hymns for children, published under her
name in Religion, Sister Mary Frances Clare. In a list of books published by Wash-
bourne of London, in 1879, twenty-one titles are assigned to the authorship of "M. F.
Cusack—The Nun of Kenmare". In 1869 she published anonymously, in the form of
"an autobiography", her first attack on the Anglican conventual revival as exemplified
in the two "Protestant Sisterhoods" to which she had belonged. The title is *Five Years
in a Protestant Sisterhood and Ten Years in a Catholic Convent*. Her restlessness in whatever situation she might find herself, which had led her from Anglicanism to Roman
Catholicism, caused her in 1884 to leave Ireland and the Poor Clares to found in
England at Nottingham, and to plant in the United States, the Sisterhood of St Joseph
of Peace, and in 1888 to return from her Roman allegiance to her parent Anglicanism.
As a rabid Protestant she wrote and lectured in both England and America against the
twin evils, Romanism and "Ritualism". Even in death she was unable to abide by her
latest choice. When her last hour came at Leamington, England, in 1899, it is alleged
that she sought and was granted reconciliation to the Church which she had in turn so
loved and so hated, so extravagantly praised and so bitterly denounced.

Superior"—probably not, as Miss Goodman seems to imply, because of lack of vocation, but rather on account of her age, which at the time when Miss Goodman wrote was nearly sixty years. The date of Miss Langston's death is unknown. In the "Profession Book" at Ascot Priory there is a note to the effect that she died in her native city, London.

Miss Langston's former subject, her faithful companion at Scutari and Balaclava and in her adventures at sea, the Novice Harriet Erskine, was one of the four Sisters of the Holy Cross who accepted the "conditions of union" by which in 1856 their Community was incorporated with the Devonport Society of Sisters of Mercy to form the Society of the Most Holy Trinity. The other members of the older Sisterhood who assented to the union were Sister Clara, the Novice Lucy Watkins, and Sister Georgiana Napier. Sister Clara had been received as a Child of the Devonport Society in 1854. Sister Lucy Watkins was received as a Child of the Second Order— her name being changed for a time to Hombeline.[1] Miss Napier was still under obligation to keep herself free to go on call to her mother. She was therefore precluded from joining the First or Second Order of the Society. But inasmuch as the Sisters of Charity of the Third Order were free to live either in Community or at home, Miss Napier was received into the Society at the time of the union as a Sister of the Holy Ghost (as the Sisters of Charity were called). Whenever possible she lived and worked at St Saviour's, Osnaburgh Street, which had become the headquarters of the Third Order, until in 1864 changed circumstances set her free to be professed as a Sister of Mercy in the First Order of the Holy Communion.[2] The enclosed life to which she aspired did not become a possibility until the death of her mother in 1883.

Before the union was finally accomplished the Sisters of the two Communities who were opposed to the union withdrew. Some, like

[1] The change was made probably because at the time of the union there was already a Sister Lucy in the Society—Lucy Prynne, the little daughter of the Vicar of St Peter's Church, Plymouth, who had been dedicated by her parents to the Religious Life in infancy and was at the time of Miss Watkins' reception into the Devonport Society a Child Oblate or "Novice of the Little Habit". When Lucy Prynne was withdrawn by her parents from the Society several years later, Miss Watkins was again known as Sister Lucy. (Cf. Goodman, *Sisterhoods in the Church of England*, pp. 159–60, 131–2.)

[2] The Sisters of the First Order were free to visit their parents once a year. The enclosed Nuns of the Second Order having at their Profession "forsaken kindred and home . . . retired wholly from the world, and sought not to return to it".

Mother Emma and Novice Margaret Anna Cusack, joined the Roman Catholic Church; some, it was said, went into other Anglican Communities. Sister Etheldreda, who had relinquished her office on Mother Emma's return from the East, "resigned . . . her Sister's cross" when the two Communities were united. Whether she was one of those who joined another Anglican Sisterhood or whether she became a Roman Catholic, is not known.

The first step towards the accomplishment of the Union was the installation of Mother Lydia as Superior of the united Communities on 21 March 1856, the Feast of St Benedict, in celebration of the Mother's thirty-third birthday. The legal formalities were not completed until the following May. On the eighteenth day of that month, Trinity Sunday, the Feast of the Title of the newly-constituted Society, the Lady Superior issued and signed the first instalment of Statutes for the rule and governance of the said "Congregation of Religious of the Society of the Most Holy Trinity". The formal consummation of the Union was postponed to 27 October, the eighth anniversary of the founding of the Devonport Society of Sisters of Mercy. On 28 October, the Feast of SS. Simon and Jude, Dr Pusey, assisted by the Reverend George Rundle Prynne, Vicar of St Peter's Church, celebrated Holy Communion in the Oratory of St Dunstan's Abbey in the presence of the Mother and Sisters of the united Communities. The Union was sealed and consummated by their receiving together the Blessed Sacrament of Unity and the subsequent acknowledgement by each of the Sisters of Mother Lydia as Abbess of St Dunstan's and Mother of the Three Rules of the Society of the Most Holy Trinity.[1]

[1] In order that one of the Sisters, who was unable to attend the ceremonies because of a broken ankle, might share in this corporate act of union, the Blessed Sacrament was carried to her in her cell after the Communion of those assembled in the Oratory. This is one of the earliest recorded instances among the Tractarians of the administration of the Holy Communion to the sick by means of the Reserved Sacrament.

13

Since 1856

Sister Clara in her reminiscences states that "the Sisters of the old foundation" who accepted the union for the "most part became Sisters of the Love of Jesus and with one exception settled at Priory of Jesus Christ at Ascot". Members of the "old foundation" who did not at once become Sisters of the Love of Jesus were Sister Georgiana Napier and the Novice Harriet Erskine. Sister Georgiana at the time of union became a Sister of Charity of the Third Order of the Society. Novice Harriet, at first received into the First Order, became at the time of her Profession in 1859 a Nun of the Order of the Sacred Heart or Love of Jesus, and was known as Sister Harriet Mary. She was the Sister of the "old foundation" who became a Sister of the Love of Jesus but did not "settle at the Priory of Jesus Christ". She died at the Priory of the Sacred Heart at Bradford-on-Avon in January 1860, before the property at Ascot was acquired.

Sister Harriet was entrusted with the training of the two Child Oblates of the Order of the Sacred Heart, "Sisters of the Little Habit"—one of them, Lucy Prynne, refined and docile, as became the daughter of the Vicar of St Peter's Church, Plymouth; the other, Aileen Murphy, the orphan of two Irish beggars, victims of the cholera epidemic of 1853, who had been adopted by Mother Lydia on the death of her parents—coarse mannered, in spite of careful training and gentle environment, endowed with a saucy Irish wit, much beloved, and precociously devout.[1] Sister Harriet Mary died of tuberculosis—*la maladie des élus*—at Bradford Priory

---

[1] There was found recently at Ascot Priory in a devotional book used by Sister Lucy Watkins—known at that time as "Child Hombeline"—an hand-illuminated card inscribed: "The Voice of the Darling Child", in which are quoted the "words spoken by little Aileen . . . when told of the inscription on the coffin" of one of the Sisters: "Arise, my love, my fair one, and come away." "Oh, should you not like to go to dear Jesus?—I should like to go." To this is added a note to the effect that "Little Aileen went to Jesus July 13, 1864". Hers was the first burial in the Priory Cemetery which had been consecrated in the preceding year by Samuel Wilberforce, Bishop of Oxford.

on 10 January 1860, in the thirty-fifth year of her age, the seventh
of her life in Religion and the first of her Profession. Shortly before her death her mother came to visit her. Dr Pusey was summoned
from Oxford to minister to her in her last hours. Her death "was very
calm and happy". "God will not let me fear", she was heard to
say. "Fear of death had been her natural temper", one of the Sisters
wrote, adding that the Vicar of Bradford "gave her the last Sacrament", after her Spiritual Father, Dr Pusey, had given her the "final
absolution". Dr Pusey also said the Prayer of Commendation,
"full of peace concerning her". "Nothing," he said "could be
more blessed. All that had grieved her had wholly disappeared."[1]
Her body was laid to rest beside the grave of her sister Nun of the
Sacred Heart who had died in Bradford in 1857, Sister Charlotte
Frideswida Richards.

In 1856 the Sisters of the Love of Jesus had left Bristol to live in
modified enclosure in a Tudor-Jacobean mansion with extensive
walled grounds at Bradford, known as the Priory of the Sacred Heart,
which was taken on lease and fitted up as a "nunnery" for the Sisters
of the Love of Jesus. Some of the Nuns were sent to tend the sick—
convalescents and incurables—in the small hospital which had been
established in 1858 in a rented house at Boyne Hill, Maidenhead.
Early in 1861 Dr Pusey wrote to Mr A. J. Beresford-Hope that "in
their present hired house [at Boyne Hill] the Sisters were not allowed
to build even a temporary additional ward", and that the Sisters at
Bradford "had to leave their present hired abode". He added that
"a very healthy piece of ground (some acres)" of heathland and pine
woods "had been bought by the Society, at Ascot" in Berkshire, and
that "there was money enough to provide the Sisters' rooms, but . . .
not enough to build the wards".

The Sisters left Bradford in 1861. At Ascot they were housed in
cottages on the grounds until the first unit of the Priory buildings could be erected—the present spacious ward with its thirty-
three beds commemorating the thirty-three years of our Lord's
earthly life. The architect was George Gilbert Scott. The plan of the
ward was drawn by Mother Lydia herself while sitting on a rock by

---

[1] Sister Harriet's last day but one on earth was troubled by the efforts of her mother,
who had steadily opposed her daughter's becoming a Sister, to persuade Sister Harriet
to alter her Will by which her share in her mother's estate was bequeathed to the
Devonport Society. Lady Erskine and the daughter who accompanied her to Bradford
left before Sister Harriet's death.

the seaside. The complete plans included cells for the resident Sisters and a conventual church. The ward was blessed by Dr Pusey on the Feast of the Finding of the Holy Cross, 3 May 1862. Legally incorporated as "The London and Ascot Convalescent Hospital", its ecclesiastical title was "The Hospital of the Holy Cross and Passion". The ward was dedicated to St Raphael. One of the cells, named Stigmata, was allotted to Sister Clara as an "anchorhold", where she continued the life of a recluse which she had begun at Bristol in 1854.

Sister Lucy Watkins, as a Child of the Second Order of the Society, manifested fanatical devotion to the letter of the Rule which was noted by Miss Goodman in her book, *Sisterhoods in the Church of England*, as was also her heroic self-control at a time of tragic family bereavement. In 1864 she succeeded Sister Bertha Turnbull in the office of Sister-in-Charge of St Saviour's, Osnaburgh Street, when Sister Bertha was sent to Hawaii. In 1876 she left the Society to work under Mrs Palmer in the Cancer Hospital which Mrs Palmer eventually continued at St Saviour's after Mr Palmer bought it from the Devonport Society. She returned to the Society in 1879. In 1890 she was appointed Sister-in-Charge of St Dunstan's Abbey and Assistant Superior of the Society. She died at the Abbey on the Eve of Lady Day, 1893, in the fortieth year of her life in Religion.

Union, once effected between the two Sisterhoods, was followed by gradual assimilation. Each of the uniting Communities had an enriching contribution to make to the resultant Society of the Most Holy Trinity. The ascetical tone and the contemplative ideal fostered by Dr Pusey in the members of the Park Village Community were fruitfully cultivated by the Nuns of the Second Order of the Society, the Sisters of the Love of Jesus. These elements were brought under sympathetic direction and needed control by Mother Lydia's adaptation for their governance of the Constitutions of the Poor Clares of the Reform of St Colette.[1] In course of time the "mixed" life of the Sisters of Mercy took on a more ascetic tone and more distinctly conventual character, due no doubt to the inspiration of the Nuns of the Love of Jesus with whom they were brought into increasingly

[1] Such "holy follies" in fasting as had cost Sister Katherine Ogilvie her life and had broken the health of Sister Jane Ellacombe were not sanctioned by the Devonport Rule. The use of other bodily austerities was carefully safeguarded from self-willed indiscretion. The discipline of silence and of what some criticized as an exaggerated emphasis on obedience were outstanding features of both the First and Second Orders, the Sisters of Mercy and the enclosed Nuns.

close association as they shared in the work of nursing the patients in the Hospital at Ascot. This gradual assimilation of the First Order to the Second, in all but designation and dress and place of residence,[1] cost the Society two of its members as already related—the Eldress Sarah Anne Terrot and the Lay Probationer Margaret Goodman. Miss Goodman infers that there were others besides herself and Miss Terrot. Miss Goodman left in 1859 on being refused admission to Profession on the ground that the Superior "considered that she should remain a longer time on probation". Miss Goodman admitted, in a letter to Miss Nightingale written shortly after her defection that she "was perhaps never adapted" for the life which she had left.

However unacceptable it may have been to some of the Sisters, the alleged change in the character of the First Order of the Devonport Society insured it a definite spirit of religious dedication distinguishing it from a group of devout women loosely bound together for practical purposes in a communal form of life for the pursuit of charitable, educational, social, and missionary activities.

Mother Lydia died on 20 November 1876. In August of the following year, 1877, St Saviour's was sold. The orphans were sent to Ascot where they were housed temporarily in buildings on the Priory grounds. In the course of time many of the Sisters of Charity, following the examples of Sister Georgiana, passed into the Second Order, some of them through temporary membership in the First.

After the death of Sister Lucy in 1893 there were in the Society of the Most Holy Trinity only two Sisters who had been members of the Park Village Community.[2] These were Sister Georgiana Napier,

[1] As need demanded there came to be less and less separation as to place of residence between the two Orders. It often became necessary for a Sister of the First Order to be sent to Ascot to help with the nursing, or for a Nun of the Second Order to be assigned to temporary residence at St Dunstan's, Abbey Mere, in Plymouth, the "official residence" of the First Order, as well as Mother House of the entire Society. The author has in his possession a water-colour sketch, the work of Sister Clara, showing the Priory as it was in 1862, in which a black-habited, white-veiled Sister of Mercy is pictured in the foreground at the right, and a brown-habited, black-veiled Nun of the Love of Jesus is seen near the Priory, apparently wheeling a patient in a Bath chair. A third group, small, and indistinct even under a magnifying glass, may be intended to represent a blue-habited Sister of Charity helping a lame patient to walk with the help of sticks.

[2] In 1893 at least four other women were living who had been Sisters of the Holy Cross: Miss Sarah Anne Terrot; Sister Mary Michael Joseph Xavier of St Joseph, O.C.D., the former Sister Caroline Augusta Colt; Miss Cusack, the sometime "Nun of Kenmare"; and Sister Margaret Esther Hooper, of the Community of St John Baptist.

who on the death of Mother Lydia's successor, Mother Bertha Turn-bull, in 1890, had been elected Superior by the Chapter of the Society, and Sister Clara of the Holy Incarnation.[1] They had both begun their Life in Religion at Park Village West in 1847.

There was, however, a Sister "settled at the Priory of Jesus Christ" at this time whose association with the older Community had begun when the Sisters of the Holy Cross were her neighbours in Albany Street—the former Miss Caroline Augusta Madox-Blackwood. Miss Madox-Blackwood, it will be remembered, had not been free at that early date to join the Sisterhood, but had found it possible in 1856 to become an extern Sister of Charity of the newly constituted Society of the Most Holy Trinity. In 1882 the death of her stepmother set her free to realize her patiently cherished desire to become a Nun of the Love of Jesus. Dr Pusey, who was fast approaching the end of his life on earth, had been distressed by a report that Sister Caroline did not intend to avail herself of her liberty to become a Nun. One of the last letters written by him was addressed to her in "searching" remonstrance. The report which gave him such distress was not true. Late in 1882, after Dr Pusey's death, Sister Caroline was received as a Novice of the Second Order of the Society and in 1884 was professed as a Nun of the Love of Jesus. In that year the castle and estate of Pitreavie were sold for the sum of £50,000. Generous shares of this amount were settled on Sister Caroline's younger sister, the wife of the Reverend E. Valentine Mason and on the Episcopal church in Dunfermline. The large sum remaining (£35,000) was devoted to the completion of the Priory Church at Ascot, of which only a fragment had been built in Dr Pusey's lifetime: one bay of the nave, completed in 1870, consisting of two Norman arches, inspired by a visit of Mother Lydia in 1867 to Iffley Church, and temporary walls to the east and west, the arches "bricked up where it was hoped that some day there would be aisles". The lofty and majestic Priory Church of Jesus Christ, built after plans furnished free of cost by William Butterfield, was completed in 1886 and blessed by Dr Pusey's successor as Warden, the Reverend R. A. J. Suckling.

In sacrificing its separate corporate identity by union with the

[1] A Sister of the Love of Jesus is permitted, "if she desire, to choose, with the approval of the Reverend Mother, a mystery of faith or devotion for her own dedication in Religion"; for example, "The Holy Incarnation", "The Passion", "The Precious Blood", "The Resurrection", "The Ascension", "The Peace of God", "The Divine Silence".

Devonport Society the Sisterhood of the Holy Cross did not lose its life, but renewed it in the lives of its members who, as "English Catholic Nuns" of the Company of the Love of Jesus, continued under the direction of Dr Pusey the quest for hidden sanctity begun under his direction in Park Village West. Worship of God in liturgical and contemplative prayer was the sustaining power and inspiration of ministry to the bodies and souls of God's bereaved, suffering, or sinful children. To these ministries the care of orphans was added in 1877 when St Saviour's was sold.

Mother Georgiana, stern towards herself, gentle towards others, endeared herself to all who knew her—Sisters, patients, orphans, those living in the world who had any association with her. Her last days on earth were spent in illness which often confined her to her bed but in no wise diminished her capacity for loving and being loved, nor dulled her Scottish humour. God "gave her rest" on 16 April 1900—the eighty-first year of her age and the fifty-fourth of her Life in Religion.

Sister Clara's old age suggested to Dr Pusey's biographer, Miss Maria Trench, the patient waiting of Anna in the temple. Her tenure of the office of Sister-in-Charge of the Priory, in which she succeeded Mother Georgiana in 1890, was distinguished alike by devotion to the needs and comfort of the patients of the hospital and the training of the orphans—and by a naïve trust in human integrity which some-times caused embarrassment beyond, as well as within, the Priory enclosure.[1] During an illness which "was supposed to be her last, she took leave of all the Sisters, saying something to each—to Sister Elizabeth [the Sister who had charge of the orphans], 'Holy, Holy, Holy'. This", commented the priest who related the incident, "falls in with a remark that 'she found recreation enough in sitting on the floor and contemplating the Blessed Trinity' ". Her illness, however, did not end in death, but in recovery. It was not until six years later, some four years after the death of Mother Georgiana, that God called Sister Clara to her rest on 12 February 1904. She was eighty-five years old and had been in Religion fifty-six years.

It was of the Priory of Jesus Christ as he knew it in the years

[1] An old friend of Sister Clara is authority for the story that "when she first became Sister-in-Charge she put up a sign at the gate [of the Priory grounds] that poor tra-vellers would be relieved. The nuisance caused by the influx of tramps made the local justices ask that the sign be removed."

1898–9, when Mother Georgiana and Sister Clara were still living, that the late Father Bartle Hack, sometime Vicar of St Mary Magdalene, Oxford, wrote to the author: "It is difficult to describe the atmosphere of the convent . . . perhaps it might be, 'Our conversation is in heaven'." The passage of time since 1900 has not brought with its other changes any difference in that atmosphere of "conversation in heaven". In fact, as Mr Peter F. Anson notes in his account of Ascot Priory in *The Call of the Cloister*, one has "the sense that time has stopped still"—not only that "one has been transported back at least eighty years", so that "one would not be surprised to meet Dr Pusey walking beside Mother Lydia's wheelchair along the paths between the rhododendron bushes", but also—for those who are sensitive to the things of the spirit—time seems to have "stopped still" in the sense of having been taken up into the "never ending now" of eternity. Father Hack noted that "there was something unearthly about the whole place. . . . Never before or since or anywhere had he seen anything like it . . . something unique and beautiful. . . . The memory of Dr Pusey was fragrant." He "did not think anything so unique and wonderful could ever come to an end". Nor has it come to an end. The devout visitor of to-day finds in the Priory of Jesus Christ the same "sense of the numinous" which impressed the devout visitor of a half-century ago—the same atmosphere of heavenly converse, of affections set not on things of earth but on things above: a sense of "homeliness with God", a spirit of "supernatural naturalness", a "holy merriness"—*sancta hilaritas*—which must be experienced to be known. All that was best in the spirit of Park Village West lives on to-day at Ascot in the Priory of Jesus Christ.

APPENDIX

I

Unsolved Problems of Identification of Sisters Named in Early Records

At the present time of writing (1964) very few of the problems of identification of early members of the Sisterhood of the Holy Cross remain unsolved. Christian charity may rejoice that the initial H conceals the surname of the aspirant of the life of a Sister of Mercy, mentioned by Miss Cusack in *Five Years* (p. 49), who left the house in high dudgeon at being given a pair of plain boots to be worn instead of the fashionable *chaussure* with which she was shod when she came to Park Village West—accompanying her reputed action of tossing the offensive footwear to, "or at" (Miss Cusack suggested), the Sister who proffered it, with "very warm" language. No less interesting, and no less evasive of identification, is the ascetically ambitious postulant (also mentioned by Miss Cusack) who, on being refused permission to emulate St Catherine of Siena by abstaining from all food except the Sacred Species received in Holy Communion, left the house in pained disillusionment when the rest of the Community sat down to dinner.

The Sisters at Ascot Priory and all others who have studied the records of the Park Village and Devonport Sisterhoods have been puzzled by a statement of Miss Cusack in *The Story of my Life* (p. 65) that a Sister named Eliza, said by Miss Cusack to have been in charge of the orphans at St Saviour's, Osnaburgh Street, in 1854, was one of the London Community who accompanied Miss Nightingale to Scutari. No such person is named as one of the party of Anglican Sisters who nursed at Scutari and Balaclava, either in Miss Terrot's *Reminiscences of Scutari Hospitals* or in the list of the same preserved at Ascot Priory. The number of Sisters of the Regent's

Park and Devonport Sisterhoods who accompanied Miss Nightingale is everywhere stated to have been *eight*. Miss Cusack gives that as the number of Sisters, omitting, however, the name of Novice Harriet Erskine—Miss Cusack's eighth being the aforesaid "Sister Eliza". Considering that Miss Cusack's account was written in 1899, some forty-five years after the events narrated, and that she adds Sister Eliza's name as an afterthought, it is not unreasonable to surmise that the name "Eliza" was substituted in her memory for "Harriet"—and that the Sister intended was Sister Harriet Erskine, who is not named by Miss Cusack. In a letter of Mother Emma Langston written in the autumn of 1854 to Mother Lydia Sellon mention is made of a Sister Eliza whose opposition to the union of the older Sisterhood with the Devonport Society "pained" Mother Emma. The context indicates that Sister Eliza was not among the Sisters *en route* to the East. Beyond these two references there is no further mention of Sister Eliza in surviving documents.

Four Sisters bearing the name of Caroline—two of them, by odd coincidence, being Scottish and having the same middle name of Augusta—are mentioned in early records of the Park Village Sisterhood. One of these has been proved by documentary evidence to have been Miss Caroline Augusta Colt of Edinburgh and Gartsherrie, whose story is told in the foregoing pages. Another was Miss Caroline Augusta Madox (later Blackwood) whose identity has been incontestably established and whose history is recorded in this history of her community. The third was Miss Caroline Paul, listed in the Census of 1851 as a "Sister of Mercy" residing at No. 17 Park Village West in that year, whose birthplace, Exeter, and her age at the time when the census was taken, together with her name comprise the sum total of what is known of her. She is nowhere mentioned in any of the records of the Park Village Sisterhood so far discovered. No trace of her can be found among the several families bearing the name of Paul listed by Burke or any other genealogists. The fourth Sister Caroline was Mother Lydia's half-sister, Patty Caroline Sellon, whose history is known and is recorded in *Priscilla Lydia Sellon*.

In 1933, when the assembly of materials for the writing of *Priscilla Lydia Sellon* was begun, the names of comparatively few of the Sisters of the Holy Cross were known, even by their "grand-daughters in Religion" at Ascot Priory. The few whose names were known were for the most part Sisters of the older Community who in 1856 or after were received into the Devonport Society either as Sisters of Mercy or Nuns of the Love of Jesus. No one at Ascot knew of Miss Cusack as having been a member of the Park Village and Devonport Sisterhoods, nor yet of Sisters Elizabeth Wilcox, Caroline Augusta Colt, Charlotte White, Helen Ind, Katherine Ogilvie, Caroline Paul, Margaret Hooper, or the Sister Harriet named in Mr Dodsworth's letters and in the Reverend W. Upton Richards' correspondence with Dr Pusey. Nor was it remembered either at Ascot or in Lloyd Square that "she who was the Foundress of the Sisters of Bethany was among the Sisters" at No. 17 Park Village West in 1847.

In the summer of 1961 letters were found among the Pusey Papers in the library of Pusey House, Oxford, establishing the identity of the Sister Helen, mentioned in a letter of Mr Dodsworth addressed to Dr Pusey in 1847, as Miss Helen Ind, an acquaintance of Miss Clarissa Powell (in Religion Sister Clara of the Holy Incarnation). The identification is fortified by references to the same Miss Ind in the diary of Mother Marian Hughes as having been sent by Dr Pusey from the Regent's Park Sisterhood to Miss Hughes' newly established Community in Oxford in the Spring of 1851, and to Miss Ind's departure from that Community in the autumn of the same year. In a letter written long after 1851 Sister Clara made inquiry if her correspondent could give her any information about "our former Sister Helen Ind". A memorandum discovered at Ascot Priory indicates that Miss Ind yielded to inducements offered by her father to abandon her aspiration to the Religious Life. In 1864 she was in friendly relations with the Sisters of the Devonport Society, but at a later date she became a Roman Catholic.

To the present Superior of the Community of St John Baptist, Clewer, thanks are due, and are herewith tendered, for access to documents relevant to the Park Village Sisterhood recently discovered by her among the archives of her own Community. Of particular interest and value are the notes of Sister Margaret Esther concerning the Park Village Community and her own connection with it.

K

NAMES OF WOMEN
KNOWN TO HAVE BEEN "AMONG THE SISTERS"
IN THE COMMUNITY OF THE HOLY CROSS
(1845–1856)

1845	Jane Isabella Ellacombe[1]	Died 1854
	Mary Bruce	Left 1847 (ill health)
	Sarah Anne Terrot	Devonport, 1848 or 1849
	Emma Rebecca Langston, (Superior 1845–55)	Devonport, 1854–Roman Catholic 1856
	Etheldreda Pillans (Superior 1855)	Left 1856
	Caroline Augusta Colt	Roman Catholic 1847
	Elizabeth Wilcox	Left 1845–Roman Catholic 1846
1846	Harriet Barrand (or Barraud)	At Devonport 1851 (as Sister Maude)
	Etheldreda Anna Benett[1][2]	Left 1846 (parental pressure)
1847	Helen Ind	Left 1851 (parental pressure)
	Georgiana Napier[1]	Associate Sister 1847–Devonport 1856
	Katherine Ogilvie[1]	Died 1850
	Clarissa Powell[1]	Devonport 1854
1848	Charlotte Cordelia White	Left 1850 or 1851–Roman Catholic
Before 1849	Susanna Logan	Devonport 1849—Left 1853–4 (ill health)
1850	Margaret Anna Cusack	Devonport 1854–Roman Catholic 1858
Unknown	Caroline Paul	Left before 1856
	Eliza	Left before 1856
(1852)	Mary Kebble (or Kebbel)	Left (duty to parents)
	Caroline Augusta Madox[1][3]	Associate Sister–left (duty to parent)
	Margaret Hooper[4]	Associate Sister–Devonport (Sister of Charity)
1854	Lucy Watkins[1]	Devonport 1856
	Harriet Erskine[1]	Devonport 1856

[1] Died as Religious of the Anglican Communion.
[2] Founded in 1864 the Society of the Sisters of Bethany.
[3] Devonport: Sister of Charity 1856; Nun of Second Order 1883.
[4] Joined the Community of St John Baptist, Clewer, in 1864. In Religion Sister Margaret Esther, C.S.J.B.

The Rule of the Sisterhood of the Holy Cross

THE SEVERAL VERSIONS OF THE RULE

The title of the Rule of the Sisterhood of the Holy Cross was *Rules for a Holy and Devoted Life Whereby to Live in Love to GOD and in Acts of Love to Him and His.* Sister Clara sent to Canon Liddon a copy of this Rule, accompanied by reminiscences of the early days of the Sisterhood in which she stated that the Rule was "said to be an adaptation of that of the Visitation". This copy sent by Sister Clara was declared by Dr Liddon to be "the first edition of the Park Village Rule . . . wanting five chapters which were probably not written out as not being wanted by Sister Clara. The second edition", he continued, "is given [among] Dr Pusey's letters to Mr Beresford-Hope." These letters and the copy of the Rule are reproduced in a bound volume of transcripts in the pamphlet room of Pusey House, Oxford. The text of the Rule from which the transcript was made is contained in a notebook, also at Pusey House, bearing on the inner side of the front cover the name A. J. B. Hope. In this notebook there is a preliminary statement explaining why Mr Beresford-Hope had in his possession a copy of the Rule of the Sisterhood: "There was trouble with Bishop Blomfield in 1847–8. During this crisis A.J.B.H. was employed by Dr Pusey as an intermediary and made peace. Towards this end he claimed to see and to show (as he did) a copy of the Rule to the Bishop. . . . Bishop Blomfield read the Rule without comment and handed it to A. J. B. Hope in the blank cover." This "second edition" of the Rule, as Canon Liddon designated it, he further described as "the original Rule revised in order to send to the Bishop of London". He added: "Sister Etheldreda (Miss Benett), who was herself at Park Village, sent a complete MS. of the first edition, the variations of which from Edition 2 are noted . . . on the pages opposite to the copy of Edition 2 sent by Mr Beresford-Hope."

The preliminary stages in the drafting of the original form of the Rule were recounted by Dr Pusey in a letter to Mr Beresford-Hope dated Quinquagesima, 1848:[1] "Lord John Manners procured us the Rules of the Sisters of [Mercy] at Birmingham. I had some Rules by me, used by different bodies in England and on the continent.[2] We took as our basis St Augustine's, as extant in an Epistle of his to some 'Sanctimoniales' whom he had brought together. . . . On this we engrafted others. . . .[3] When this was done, Dodsworth and myself looked over it, with a view to what the Bishop of London would think; and several little points were altered (chiefly language) on his saying, 'The Bishop would not like that'. This we kept to be shown to the Bishop, whenever trial enough had been made of the institution for him to be ready to take it up. . . . When we had thus reviewed the Rules we showed them to J. Keble."[4]

The Rule, as reviewed and revised by Dr Pusey and Mr Dodsworth in 1845 in the manner described above, was the "original edition" of which Mother Ethel Benett sent a "complete manuscript" to Canon Liddon, and of which Sister Clara's copy is a slightly abbreviated version. This was the Rule by which the Sisterhood was governed from its inauguration in 1845 until the "trouble with Bishop Blomfield in 1847 and 1848" led Mr Beresford-Hope to advise further revision with an eye to the Rule being submitted to the Bishop. To this proposal Dr Pusey assented. "As you suggest," he wrote in reply to Mr Beresford-Hope, "we will again review [the Rules], and since the Bishop is willing to see them, would most gladly submit them to him."

[1] Cf. p. 15 above.

[2] Foremost among the continental Rules were the Constitutions and Spiritual Directory of the Nuns of the Visitation and of the Ursuline Nuns of Bayeux. The leather-bound manuscript copy of the Ursuline Rule, Constitutions, and Spiritual Directory, treasured among the relics of Mother Marian Hughes by the Sisters of the Holy and Undivided Trinity, was probably one source of Dr Pusey's knowledge of continental Rules.

[3] Notably the Constitutions and Spiritual Directory of the Visitation Nuns and of the Roman Catholic Sisters of Mercy.

[4] On 28 August 1845 Mr Keble wrote to Dr Pusey: "The other day Dodsworth was so good as to lend me the Rules of the Sisterhood in London, and we, *i.e.* I and my wife, were deeply interested in them." It was at this time, no doubt, that Mr and Mrs Keble made the transcript of the Rule found many years later by Miss Trench, as related below.

Miss Cusack, in *Five Years in a Protestant Sisterhood* (pp. 36–7) gave a detailed account of a revision of the Rule which, she claimed, was made in anticipation of its being shown to the Bishop "about four years" after the Sisterhood had been established.[1] The omissions and alterations said by Miss Cusack to have been made at the revision reported by her are identical with the omissions and alterations which differentiate the Beresford-Hope version from Mother Ethel's manuscript of the "first edition".

This "Complete Manuscript of the Original Rule" sent by Mother Ethel has not been located. The original Rule is represented, however, in a slightly altered form, by the copy sent by Sister Clara to Canon Liddon, as noted above, as well as by the marginal notes in the transcription of Mr Beresford-Hope's copy at Pusey House. In one of the manuscript accounts of the Sisterhood of the Holy Cross found at Ascot Priory there is a note to the effect that at the time of the union "St Saviour's became the home of the Third Order—of the Holy Ghost—with the Rule of the Holy Spirit [a slip of the pen for "Holy Cross"?] altered, though still very strict".

There is also at Ascot Priory a copy of the Rule entitled *A Manuscript Rule of Dr Pusey's Making for the Sisterhood of the Holy Cross, Regent's Park (1845)*. This version is shorter by seven chapters than the revision of 1848. It differs in many other particulars from that version and from the original Rule, as represented by Sister Clara's copy and the marginal notes indicating the variations of the Beresford-Hope transcription from Mother Ethel's manuscript. It does, however, omit the chapter "Of Confesson" and the supposedly "objectionable" passages in the Chapter "Of Holy Communion". For these reasons the Ascot manuscript may be reckoned a "revised version" of the Beresford-Hope revision of 1848. As such it does not require separate consideration. It may be the copy "for private use" said to have been at one time at Ascot, but is *not* the copy sent by Sister Clara to Canon Liddon.

Sister Clara stated in her reminiscences that, besides the "copy for private use" at that time at Ascot, there was another copy "in the hands of Miss Trench ... said to have been penned by Mr Keble",

---

[1] If the revision described by Miss Cusack was that of 1848, her "four years" would be actually only three. However, the vagueness of her term of reckoning—"about four years"—makes it possible to assign her revision to 1848. The chronological difficulty involved in the identification of the revision reported by Miss Cusack with the revision of 1848 is considered below.

and a third at Christ Church. Of the copy "said to have been penned by Mr Keble" Miss Trench related that "she found a paper among several of Mr Keble's, written partly in his hand and partly in Mrs Keble's, which seemed as if it must have been the Rule of some Society. She took it to [Sister Clara] and asked her if she could tell her what it was". "I can see her now," added Miss Trench, "turning over the pages with eager, trembling fingers as she exclaimed, 'I do believe it is our old Rule at St Saviour's'!"[1] Miss Trench entertained the belief that this was the original Rule and that it was the composition of Mr Keble. This belief, Mother Bertha assured Canon Liddon, "was not correct. It was only Miss Trench's fancy, because she found it amongst Mr Keble's papers. Dr Pusey sent the copy to him to look over". The copy said to be at Christ Church has not been available for inspection by the authors of this work. Nor have they seen the Keble transcript.

A hand-illuminated copy of the Rule as revised in 1848 was recently found in the archives of the Community of St John Baptist at Clewer, which was the basis of the Clewer Rule given in a manuscript volume found at the same time, entitled *The Founder's Rule Book*. Another copy of the version of 1848 is contained in a locked leather-bound volume, also at Clewer, containing notes of the Park Village Community and the Third Order (Sisters of Charity of the Holy Ghost) of the Devonport Society, compiled by Miss Margaret Hooper, who was an Associate Sister of the Holy Cross before the Sisterhood was absorbed by the Devonport Society, and a Sister of Charity in the latter, before her admission in 1864 as Novice Margaret Esther to the Community of St John Baptist. Besides much interesting, and some important, information about the Regent's Park Sisterhood, Sister Margaret Esther noted in detail the changes made in the Park Village Rule when it was adapted for the governance of the "Sisters in residence" at St Saviour's, in 1856. A printed copy of this adaptation was found by one of the authors of this work in the coffer, now at Ascot Priory, which once stood in the chancel of the Oratory of St Dunstan's Abbey, Plymouth, as described by Miss Goodman in *Sisterhoods in the Church of England* (p. 34). This printed version is entitled *Obligations of the Sisters of the Holy Ghost, together*

---

[1] Miss Trench noted that Sister Clara remarked, "Ah, we should have done well if we had kept this! But we all fancy that 'Paradise is next door'. I thought the Devonport Society was Paradise." (See Chapter 8, page 86, above.)

with the Long Rule or Rules of the Sisters in Residence. Sister Clara, in a memorandum recording the union of the Sisters of the Holy Cross with the Devonport Society in 1856, stated that when Mother Lydia Sellon was "recognized as Superior" by the Sisters of the Holy Cross who were in favour of the union, "she modified the Rule" of the older Community and established the Sisters of the Holy Ghost at St Saviour's "on the old foundation". The Rule, thus modified and designated "The Long Rule", was observed by the Sisters only when they were "in residence" at St Saviour's. In their own homes (and probably in the Mission House in the East End) they kept a short, simple Rule, known as "Obligations of the Sisters of the Holy Ghost".

Sister Clara's statement has been quoted to the effect that the Rule of the Park Village Community was "said to be an adaptation of that of the Visitation". Miss Langston in reply to an inquiry addressed to her by Miss Cusack after they had both left the Sisterhood and the Church of England, asserted that the Rule which they had followed in the Regent's Park Community "was strictly speaking a compilation from the Nuns of the Visitation founded by St Francis de Sales. For the most part it was taken word for word from the authorized English translation ... Our Rule", she continued, "was the original Rule and Spiritual Directory *messed* together. The Constitutions were left out entirely". A comparison of the several versions of the Rule of the Sisterhood of the Holy Cross with the authorized English translation of *The Rules of St Augustin: With the Constitutions and Directory Composed for the Religious Sisters of the Visitation* (London, 1803), verifies Sister Clara's and Miss Langston's statements about the basic source of the Park Village Rule, but does not support Miss Langston's allegation that "the Constitutions were left out entirely". Rather does such a comparison reveal that several of the chapters of the Holy Cross Rule were either taken over wholly or in part, or adapted, from the Constitutions of the Visitation, as many others were derived from the Spiritual Directory and from the Rule of St Augustine. The rules regulating the external activities of the Sisters in the school, in visiting, and in the care of orphans and "distressed women" were adapted from the Rule and Constitutions of the Roman Catholic Sisters of Mercy.[1]

[1] Quotation has already been made of Dr Pusey's letter to Mr Beresford-Hope in which he stated that a copy of these Rules and Constitutions had been obtained for

THE CONTENT OF THE RULE

The Rule of the Sisterhood of the Holy Cross is described by Canon
Liddon on pages 23 and 24 of Volume III of his *Life of E. B. Pusey*
as consisting "in its complete form of thirty-three chapters, which
are not so much a dry code of directions as a series of spiritual exhortations"—"short sermons" the Reverend W. J. Butler called them
in a letter addressed to Dr John Mason Neale in 1855.

The first chapter, entitled "Of the Object of the Institute", was
taken with slight verbal alterations from the Rule and Constitutions
of the Roman Catholic Sisters of Mercy. The object was declared to be
"to afford opportunities to persons apart from the world and its
distractions to perfect holiness in the fear of God, and to grow in the
love of our Lord and Saviour Jesus Christ, especially in cherishing
and showing forth love to Him in his poor and afflicted brethren".
To this end the Sisters were exhorted to "lay aside all secondary
matter, all love of self . . . and make the love of Christ the end" of
all they did, their "support, strength, strong hope and exceeding
great reward. . . . To offer up the performance of every duty and
every action to Christ". They would "ordinarily devote six hours
in each day to works of mercy unless any adequate occasion should
arise for omitting or enlarging the duty as charity or prudence might
require".[1] On the days when the Holy Communion was celebrated
the Sisters were to be "dispensed from active duties, except those
which were urgently needed, in order to cherish inward recollection
. . . as also for fitting relaxation of body and mind". The Sisters were
to "study more and more to meditate on the Passion, especially on
each Friday, and out of love to it, to bear more cheerfully any pains,
slights, or sufferings" which might befall them. Thanksgiving or
preparation for Holy Communion was to "form a chief part of each
day's devotion". Especially after Holy Communion the Sisters were
directed to "spend some time in thanksgiving. . . . When the Holy

---

him by Lord John Manners. In January, 1845 Bishop (later Cardinal) Wiseman sent
to Dr Pusey "The Order of the Day" as set forth for the Sisters of Mercy of Birmingham, and in 1846, immediately before the beginning of Lent, he wrote again, giving the
"dietary" of the Birmingham Sisters. (Liddon, *Life of E. B. Pusey*, Vol. III, p. 22;
[Trench] *Story of Dr Pusey's Life*, pp. 272–3.)

[1] Many years later Dr Pusey stated that "in the early days" six hours of work was
"found to be too much".

Eucharist was not celebrated [they were directed] to make at least once in the day an act of Spiritual Communion."

Thirty-two additional chapters follow, which were thus summarized by Canon Liddon:

> The various Christian graces of humility, charity, modesty and purity, voluntary poverty and obedience are insisted on, and practical directions are given for the cultivation of them. There follow the various elements of the devotional side of the Christian Life: attendance at the offices of the Church, Holy Communion, the practice of self-examination, confession, meditation or mental prayer, and mortification or fasting. The daily life of a Sister is next provided for by rules for the intentions or purpose with which she is to perform the successive actions of the day: for silence at certain hours, as befitting souls which have fixed their gaze on God; for the management of thoughts during silent employments; for the avoidance of inquisitiveness or meddlesomeness; for intercourse with persons outside the Sisterhood; and for times of recreation. Directions are given for admitting new Sisters, for the conduct of the Superior, and for the life of the Lay Sisters, thus providing for the religious organization of the Society. The rest of the Rule may be described as a series of appendices concerned with the details of daily life and work. The last portion is devoted to the works of mercy which the Sisterhood was to undertake: visiting the sick, teaching in schools, the admission of distressed women to a temporary home, and the distribution of time among these several occupations.

"The Rule in its complete form," on which Canon Liddon based the preceding summary, seems to have been "the complete manuscript of the first edition of the Rule" sent to him by Mother Ethel Benett, inasmuch as he included in his summary the chapter "Of Confession", which was "suppressed altogether" in the revision of 1848 and is missing from the Beresford-Hope version, from the copy sent by Sister Clara, from the illuminated copy at Clewer, and from the *Manuscript Rule* at Ascot. Other deviations from Mother Ethel's manuscript are noted below. Miss Cusack's account of a revision in which these alterations were said to have been made is given on p. 143.

THE RULE IN DETAIL

The first chapter of the Rule, summarized in the preceding section of this appendix, is followed by a chapter entitled "Of Humility", based on the Constitutions of the Visitation Nuns. Chapter III, "Of Union and Charity" is taken from the Rule of St Augustine. The chapter "Of Modesty and Purity" in Mother Ethel's "first edition" begins with an exhortation, from the Constitutions of the Visitation, "to live, breathe, pant for your celestial Spouse", which was omitted from the revision of 1848 on the obvious ground that "the Bishop would not like that". Lacking also from the revised versions are the detailed directions given in the original for the conduct of the Sisters when away from the house: carriage of the head, custody of the eyes, especially in regard to men; calm composure and avoidance of vehemence—with quaintly specific reference to "pulling the bell".

The chapter "Of Poverty" contains in the original version a provision, derived from the Visitation Constitutions, exempting the furnishings of the Oratory from the simplicity required in all the versions for other parts of the house. In the chapter entitled "Of Obedience" is the direction: "At the voice of the Superior or the sound of the bell, be ready, as if it came from Jesus Christ, to leave whatsoever ye are about." This is altered in the revisions by the omission of the words, "as if it came from Jesus Christ", obviously, again, on the ground that "the Bishop would not like that"—as later (in 1852) Bishop Phillpotts was disturbed by the report that Mother Lydia Sellon has used like words in regard to her commands.[1] There are other minor omissions in the revised versions of this chapter.

The chapter entitled in the revisions "Of Common Prayer" was in Mother Ethel's copy of the original headed "Of the Divine Office"—a term not current in Anglican usage at that period. In the later versions, the salutary directions of the original, derived from the Visitation Constitutions, to "pronounce the words clearly and distinctly, to keep the pauses and accents moderate and adapt the voices one to another", is omitted, and the words "the voice of your heavenly Spouse" (taken from the Spiritual Directory of the Visitation) are altered to "the voice of your Lord"—still another instance of concession to the anticipated objections of Bishop Blomfield.

The chapter "Of Holy Communion" was subjected in revision to more drastic alteration than any other section of the Rule. The character, extent, and evident cause of these changes can best be appreciated through comparing the text of Mother Ethel's manuscript,

[1] *Priscilla Lydia Sellon*; J. Spurrell, *Miss Sellon and the Sisters of Mercy*, p. 17; Miss E. J. Whately, *The Anglican Sister of Mercy*, p. 127.

which followed closely the Spiritual Directory of the Visitation, with the revised text.

Mother Ethel's Manuscript
(and Sister Clara's copy)

CHAPTER VIII
Of Holy Communion

Let your principal intention in approaching the Holy Communion be to procure glory to our Lord and to yourselves increased union with Him. Now that ye be the better prepared for It, it will be proper that, on the preceding evening in your meditation and recollection time, ye fix your thoughts in some degree on our Blessed Lord as giving Himself in the Blessed Sacrament, exciting in your souls a holy reverence and a spiritual joy for being so happy as to receive the sweet Saviour. This should be attended with a fresh resolution of serving Him with fervour, which resolution you may, after receiving Him, confirm, not by vow, indeed, but by a repetition of this good and holy purpose.

When on the point of receiving ye may vocally or mentally use some devout ejaculations, e.g., "Who am I and Who art Thou?" or "Whence is this happiness to me, that my Lord should come to me?" or "Amen, come Lord Jesus", or with the Spouse, "Let Him kiss me with the kisses of His Divine Mouth".

After Holy Communion view with the eyes of faith our Lord as sitting in your heart, which is now become like a throne to Him, and summon all your powers and senses to pledge your allegiance to Him and to receive His commands.

Ye may also call forth to your soul a variety of other holy affections; e.g., of fear of grieving and losing our Lord, saying with David, "Lord, depart not from me", "Abide with me". Of confidence and fortitude of mind, "I will fear no evil, for

Revised Text

CHAPTER VIII
Of Holy Communion

Let your principal intention in approaching the Holy Communion be to grow in conformity with your Lord and in increased union with Him. Now that ye may be the better prepared for It, it will be proper that, on the preceding evening in your meditation and recollection time, ye fix your thoughts in some degree on our Blessed Lord as giving himself in the Blessed Sacrament, putting aside (unless love require it) all subjects which may distract you, and preparing yourself to receive Him by sorrow for past sin, faith, love, and purpose of serving Him with renewed fervour. This resolution ye should after Holy Communion renew.

When on the point of receiving ye may vocally or mentally use some devout ejaculations. e.g., "Who am I and Who art Thou?" or "Whence is this happiness to me, that my Lord should come to me?" or "Amen, come, Lord Jesus", or the like.

Thou art with me". Of love with the Spouse, "My beloved is mine and I am His". Of thanksgiving. Of purpose to serve Him, "The Lord shall be my God and this heart of mine which once was as hard as stone shall now be a habitation for Him".

The inward affections which arose in the soul of the Mother of God, upon being told by the angel that the Holy Ghost should come upon her, may also be thought of and imitated; viz., her ardour, her devotion, her humility, her confidence, her courage, and the oblation she made of her heart to God, as soon as she heard that God had given her His, that is, His Son, as also the love with which this holy soul became then so dissolved that she could well say, "My soul melted when my Beloved spake unto me". Now, as to us, not unlike is the favour which we receive in the Holy Communion. For we are assured, not by an angel but by Jesus Christ Himself that in this sweet mystery the Holy Ghost comes and is as it were conceived and born within us (Galatians 4:19). O God, what sweet loving kindness! And therefore how justly can a soul which is impressed with it, say with this Holy Virgin, "Behold the handmaid of the Lord. Be it unto me according to Thy Word". Justly, I say, since He, with His own Sacred Mouth declared that all who eat Him abide in Him, that they shall live for Him and in Him, and that they shall not taste death forever.

At each Communion have some special intention; for example, ask for grace to conquer some temptation, to bear patiently some afflication, to obtain the blessing of a happy death, and the like, and to make some corresponding offering to God, as that ye will be diligent in watching over this or that occasion in which your infirmity shows itself, and to do this or that with all the fervour that you can, and the like.

At each Communion pray for some special grace: as to conquer some temptation, or your besetting fault, to bear patiently some affliction, to obtain the blessing of perseverance to the end to die in the Lord and the like, and to make some corresponding offering to God, as that ye will be diligent in watching over this or that occasion in which your infirmity shows itself and to do this or that with all the fervour that you can, and the like.

The opening paragraph of this chapter "Of Holy Communion", as it stood in the original version, regulated the frequency and the occasions of the Sisters' communions in the following terms: "Ye shall communicate on Sundays and Holidays [*sic*]. Should any of you wish to communicate besides these days, ye shall have the advice of your Spiritual Guide. As to the sick who can not well come to the church, the Blessed Sacrament shall be administered to them every week, provided the nature of their disorder allows it." In the revised text, this paragraph is transferred to the end of the chapter, with a significant change in the wording of the final provision; to wit, "Besides the days on which the Holy Eucharist is celebrated in the church, ye may, with the sanction of your Spiritual Guide, receive Communion with the sick poor whom ye visit."

The following chapter, "Of the Examination of Conscience", gives directions for self-examination twice daily, with detailed suggestions for this exercise based on the Spiritual Directory. Provision was also made for the practice of the "Particular Examen". There was no mention in this chapter of the "use" of sacramental confession. Directions for such confession were given in a chapter entitled "Of Confession", which is missing entirely from the revised texts and from the Ascot *Manuscript Rule*. The reason for its suppression at the "review" of 1848 is obvious: there could be no doubt in the mind of the "reviewers" that "the Bishop would not like that".

In the chapter entitled "Of Dress and Bedding", only the Sisters' dress is actually mentioned. The Sisters were to "wear black clothing as simple as possible as to material and form. They should neither wear superfluous trimmings nor anything else which did not denote religious simplicity."

The chapter entitled "Of the Superior" was taken from the Rule of St Augustine. The chapter "Of the Domestic Sisters" enacted that the Lay Sisters "should by no means be treated differently from the others as to clothes, bedding, eating and drinking, or as to taking care of their health or providing suitable exercises for their spiritual improvement". They were to be "dealt with by the Superior and the other Sisters . . . with equal love, as being like Martha and Mary true sisters and the well-beloved of the Lord". The state of these Sisters was declared to be "very similar to that which our humble Redeemer made choice of in this world, who dedicated Himself to the service of others without ever requiring to be served Himself".

In the chapter treating "Of Admission of Sisters" the hope was expressed that "all who entered the Sisterhood would have previously weighed within themselves the holiness of the life to which they had been called. Yet in order that the Sisters might enter it with deeper conviction and a more devoted purpose . . . they should . . . during the last week previous to their admission be separated from active duties and give themselves . . . to a searching review of their past life, to meditation and prayer. Those who . . . wished to engage in this mode of life should during this probation be instructed to study these rules in order that they might weigh anew before God whether they felt an ardent desire for that frame of mind which it was the object of those rules to promote. . . ."[1]

The chapter "On Recreation", abbreviated from the Visitandine Spiritual Directory, recommended that the conversation at Recreation be "on agreeable, pious, and cheerful subjects". To that end the Sisters were exhorted to "read sufficiently to contribute to the conversation". The Rule "Of Meals", quoting from the Spiritual Directory, counselled the Sisters "never to retire from table without having mortified themselves in some slight thing, and yet without scruple . . . to eat and drink what was provided . . . accepting from the hand of God indifferently what one liked or what one did not like". Directions for the conduct of Sisters during illness and the due care of the Superior for their bodily and spiritual needs were given in the chapter entitled "Of the Care of the Sick".

The Rule treating "Of Intercourse with Those out of the Sisterhood" reminded the Sisters that, as the main object of their Institution was "that its members should attend before the Lord without distraction", they must "take great care that none of their intercourse [with persons outside the Community] be such as to distract them from thoughts of heavenly things". Parents, "or such as had stood in the place of parents", as also brothers, sisters, and other close relatives, "and (with the advice of the Spiritual Guide . . .) former female friends, were to be admitted to see any of the Sisters . . .

---

[1] This provision of the Rule for a pre-admission Retreat is interesting in the light of the account given by Miss Cusack of the "Retreat" made by her in preparation for her admission as a Probationer in 1850. (See Chapter 6, page 70, above.) It will be remembered that Sister Clara had the privilege of a Retreat at No. 17 Park Village West, in the Lent of 1847, in remote preparation for her admission to the Sisterhood at Michaelmas of that year. (See Chapter 4, page 48, above.)

during the hours of recreation". Correspondence by letter was to be restricted to "those above named", except by special sanction of the Spiritual Guide. The Superior was to receive all incoming mail and "in any doubtful case she should inquire of the Sister to whom the latter was addressed whether it be from one with whom correspondence was sanctioned. . . . No Sister was to speak to persons who might call at the Sisterhood . . . without . . . leave from the Superior" or her deputy. A final warning was given: "Since in every way the world endeavours to steal in upon those who have outwardly quitted it, in all circumstances ye shall resist all curiosity about things merely secular, and shall suppress such communications from others. . . . It shall be your object . . . to know nothing which does not relate to the Glory of God or good will towards men."[1]

In a chapter, entitled "Of Works", the Sisters were warned to take care to "prevent the spirit of devotion being smothered by inordinate fondness for outward work". The chapter "Of the Orphans" is concerned, as its title indicates, with the admission, care, and training of orphan girls. It was thought to be inspired by the rules of the Nuns of Port Royal for the management of orphans. It was actually derived from the regulations of the Roman Catholic Sisters of Mercy. The chapter "Of Visiting the Poor" is really concerned with ministry to the sick. "In the persons of the suffering poor the Sisters were to love and reverence Christ, 'who for our sakes . . . became poor'."

The directions given in the chapter "Of the School" followed closely the wording of the corresponding rule of the Sisters of Mercy. The Sisters were bidden "when they entered the school to raise their hearts to God, recommending to His protection themselves and the children committed to their care". The children were to be taught simple acts of devotion to be used on waking and through the day. The Sisters were to be diligent in catechizing and in teaching their pupils the mysteries of the Faith and the Commandments, and "to instruct them in self-examination and how to perform it faithfully". They were to "bestow much pains in preparing the children for the

---

[1] Miss Cusack stated that the Sisters did not "take in" any newspapers during her "five years in a Protestant Sisterhood". There is a memorandum by Sister Clara to the effect that at Park Village West "the seclusion was so perfect one of the Sisters knew not of the French Revolution [of 1851] or that Napoleon [III] was on the throne of France".

holy ordinance of Confirmation, as making them yet further temples
of the Holy Ghost, and for the Holy Eucharist as the means of intimate union with their Saviour through the Gift of Himself, His Body
and Blood, to them."

The two concluding chapters of the Beresford-Hope version of
the Rule are entitled, respectively, "Of the Admission of Distressed
Women" and "Of Distribution of Time". The former, adapted from
the Rule and Constitutions of the Sisters of Mercy, made provision
for "distressed women of good character [to be] admitted to the
Institute", where they were to be "instructed ... in the principal
mysteries of religion, and in their duties to God and man". Employment was to be provided for them "proportionate to their abilities".
Although they were to be "allowed to continue in this work long
enough to establish a character for good conduct", they were not to
be "encouraged to remain long in the Institute since in most cases it
would be better for them to enter soon upon the ... employment by
which they would gain their livelihood. . . . The daughters of reduced
tradesmen ... might be admitted on good recommendation ... and
allowed to remain in the house until they should have learned the
duties of a servant, and had established a claim to a recommendation
from the Institute."

The final chapter, "Of Distribution of Time", is a minute timetable of the actions of the Sisters' day, based on the Constitutions
of the Visitation Nuns. There are slight differences in wording, as
also the distribution of early morning duties, between the several
revised texts and the version given by Canon Liddon in *The Life
of E. B. Pusey*, Vol. III, p. 24. Both differ from the account given
by Miss Cusack in *Five Years* (p. 26) quoted in Chapter 3 of the
present work (pp. 37–8 above). Canon Liddon's timetable probably
represents the original arrangement as given in Mother Ethel's
manuscript of the unrevised Rule, since the traditional names of the
Little Hours of the Breviary are used, whereas in the revised versions
Prime was designated "Prayers for the First Hour", etc. The traditional names of Mattins, Lauds, Vespers, and Compline were retained. There is not sufficiently important difference between the
Liddon and Beresford-Hope timetables and the schedule outlined
by Miss Cusack to justify reproduction of these variants in tabulated
form.

All copies of the Rule seen by the authors of this work are concluded, as are all forms of the Rule of St Augustine,[1] with the following hortatory epilogue:

> Now that ye may often look into this as into a mirror and nothing be neglected through forgetfulness it shall be read to you every week, and whenever ye find that ye do that which is within it, give thanks to the Lord, the dispenser of all gifts, but wheresoever anyone among ye [*sic*] becomes conscious of having failed in any part of it, let her repent from the past and be on her guard for the future, praying God that her offences may be forgiven her and that she may not be led into temptation. Amen.

MISS CUSACK'S ACCOUNT OF
A REVISION OF THE RULE OF THE
SISTERHOOD OF THE HOLY CROSS

Miss Margaret Anna Cusack became a Probationer of the Sisterhood of the Holy Cross during the summer of 1850. In her anonymous autobiography, *Five Years in a Protestant Sisterhood and Ten years in a Catholic Convent*, published in 1869, there is an account of a revision of the Rule of the Sisterhood in which it is implied that the revision was made when she was resident in the Community and that she was personally involved in the proceedings. In her account of the Rule whose revision she was recording, Miss Cusack quoted Miss Langston, the former Superior of the Sisterhood, as stating in reply to an inquiry addressed to her by Miss Cusack: "Our Rule was, strictly speaking, a compilation from the Nuns of the Visitation. . . . For the most part it was taken, word for work, from the authorized English translation. . . . Our Rule was the original Rule and Spiritual Directory *messed* together. The Constitutions were left out entirely. We afterwards, with much thought and pains, modified Constitutions from these, with some trifling alterations to meet our external work; but [Dr Pusey?] rejected them entirely, because they contained a proviso for an appeal to the Bishop of the diocese, in case the Spiritual Father and the Superior could not agree on any point or matter of importance."[2]

Miss Cusack's account of the revision of the Rule which she claimed

---

[1] E.g., *The Bridlington Dialogue*, a commentary on the Rule of St Augustine, edited by Sister Penelope, C.S.M.V.

[2] *Five Years*, pp. 30–1.

L

was made "about four years" after the Sisterhood had been established is given on pages 36 and 37 of *Five Years*:

> The Catholic Rule, adapted and Protestantized sufficiently for the Sisters, was read by them daily. . . . [Having been] doctored for the benefit of the Sisters, it had to go through another course of doctoring for the benefit of the Bishop, who was supposed to be by no means so advanced or so enlightened as might have been expected from the responsible and grave charge which he held. . . . After [the Sisterhood] had been established about four years, the Bishop of the diocese, very naturally and properly, wished to know something of their Rule. He applied to the clergyman whose church they attended, as Dr [Pusey], their founder and director, did not belong to his diocese. His Lordship little knew what consternation he caused. On Maunday [*sic*] Thursday (I can never forget it) Mr [Dodsworth?] entered and summoned me to the Oratory. It was the first great shock in what had been till then a most happy dream. He went up to the altar and took away the beautifully bound copy of our Rule which lay thereon, saying, "This Rule must be altered before it is read again in the Oratory; it will not do to read it in its present form". I had heard nothing of the Bishop's application then, but imagined the difficulties emanated from [Mr Dodsworth], who was our temporal superintendent and had taken little or no cognizance of our spiritual affairs.[1] We were in sorrowful consternation until the next day, till [Dr Pusey] appeared; but he did not comfort us much. He went through the Rule with us, striking out different passages, altering others, and suppressing the Rule headed Confession altogether. The objectionable passages were such as implied that we were spouses of our Lord; were completely separated from the world, etc. When he observed our great grief, and had to meet my warm remonstrances, he told us that we knew the Rule well by this time, and could always keep in mind, when it was read, the parts omitted, and that he had no idea of our giving up confession, although it must not appear in the Rule.

Miss Cusack stated that the revision which she reported was made "about four years" after the Sisterhood had been established; that the events accompanying the revision took place on a Maundy Thursday and Good Friday. The vagueness of her reckoning of the number of years—"about four years", instead of the actual three—makes it possible to assign the revision the events reported to 1848. It was in

---

[1] If the revision described was that of 1848, the "temporal superintendent" of the Sisterhood was Mr Dodsworth, of whom it could not be truly or justly said that he "took no cognizance of the [Sisters'] spiritual affairs".

1848 that Mr Beresford-Hope submitted to Bishop Blomfield a copy of the Rule as revised by Dr Pusey and Mr Dodsworth in which the passages reported by Miss Cusack to have been omitted or altered are either missing or appear in a form different from the text of Mother Ethel Benett's manuscript of the original Rule and Sister Clara's copy. The chapter "Of Confession", stated by Miss Cusack to have been "suppressed altogether", is missing from the Beresford-Hope copy. The passages "such as implied that [the Sisters] were spouses of Our Lord", said to have been omitted as "objectionable", are likewise missing from the revised versions.

The identity of the omissions and alterations cited by Miss Cusack with the omissions and alterations made in the review of 1848 seems to establish the identity of the revision reported by Miss Cusack with the revision represented by the Beresford-Hope copy and the Clewer versions. The only objection which can be opposed to this identification is the fact that Miss Cusack is represented as having had a part in proceedings which took place two years before she came to Park Village West. She did not enter the Sisterhood until the summer of 1850, whereas the events which she reported took place in the Spring of 1848. The only plausible solution of the difficulty seems to be to conclude that Miss Cusack, forgetting "inverted commas" and other indications that she was quoting, was in fact quoting the first-hand account of one of the Sisters—most likely Mother Emma herself—who did have an active part in the proceedings of Maundy Thursday and Good Friday 1848.

NOTE ON THE
RELATION OF THE RULE OF A
RELIGIOUS COMMUNITY TO
ITS CONSTITUTIONS

"Rules in Religion point out the means of becoming perfect in God's service; and Constitutions indicate how these means are to be used; for example, such a Rule prescribes that prayers be sedulously attended to, and the Constitutions particularize the time, the quantity, and the quality of the prayers that are to be performed. The Rule orders that men should not be looked at indiscreetly, and the Constitutions teach that, to put this rule into execution, you are in certain occurrences to keep your eyes cast down and your faces veiled. To be short, the Rule tells what is to be done, and the Constitutions how to do it."[1]

NOTE ON ASSOCIATE SISTERS

It has been recently discovered that there were affiliated with the Sisterhood of the Holy Cross, women known as "Associate Sisters", who were "Tertiaries" rather than "Associates" in the sense in which that word is now used of women (and men) who are linked by bonds of prayer and temporal assistance with the various Religious Communities of the Anglican Communion. A reference to Sister Georgiana Napier as having been at one time (1847–56) an "Associate Sister" of the Park Village Community was thought to be an ananchronism. There was found, however, at Clewer in 1962, in the locked book already referred to, a transcription of the Rule of the "Associate Sisters of the Sisterhood of the Holy Cross" made in 1852. Of these Sisters the Rule states that "their office is to assist the Sisters (1) By Prayer, observing as far as may be in their power the Canonical Hours, and at the same times . . . as they are observed in the Sisterhood, saying the Service for Unity used by the Sisterhood on Friday after Terce" and a prayer for the Community. The Associate Sisters were not to be called "Sister" outside the Sisterhood itself. It was to this group that Sister Georgiana belonged. Documents recently discovered at Ascot Priory contain references to other women who were Associate Sisters of the Park Village Community.

[1] From *The Rules of St Augustin: with the Constitutions and Directory Composed for Religious Sisters of the Visitation by St Francis de Sales*. Translated into English from the French Edition printed at Paris. Herrisant, An. 1782. London: Keating, Brown, and Keating. Printers to the R.R. Vicars Apostolic, 37 Duke Street, Grosvenor Square. 1803.—Preface, p. xiii.

Index